LOTTA. 1867

TROUPERS

OF THE

GOLD COAST

OF THE

THE RISE OF
LOTTA CRABTREE

CONSTANCE ROURKE

FOREWORD BY JAMES WILSON

Skyhorse Publishing

First Skyhorse Publishing, Inc. edition, 2016

Skyhorse Publishing books may be purchased in bulk at special discounts for sales promotion, corporate gifts, fund-raising, or educational purposes. Special editions can also be created to specifications. For details, contact the Special Sales Department, Skyhorse Publishing, 307 West 36th Street, 11th Floor, New York, NY 10018 or info@skyhorsepublishing.com.

Skyhorse® and Skyhorse Publishing® are registered trademarks of Skyhorse Publishing, Inc.®, a Delaware corporation.

Visit our website at www.skyhorsepublishing.com.

10 9 8 7 6 5 4 3 2 1

Library of Congress Cataloging-in-Publication Data is available on file.

Cover design by Rain Saukas

Print ISBN: 978-1-63450-682-3
Ebook ISBN: 978-1-63450-683-0

Printed in the United States of America

FOREWORD

THE STORY OF LOTTA CRABTREE IS THE QUINTESSENTIAL AMERICAN narrative. Born to immigrant parents and raised among gamblers, miners, and prostitutes, Lotta ascended the economic and social ranks, and though she never married, she was courted by a host of wealthy admirers from San Francisco to New York. When she died at age seventy-seven, her estate, which had accumulated from shrewd investments in ventures such as real estate and racehorses, was valued at more than four million dollars (or roughly sixty million in 2016 dollars). Her story is also the quintessential American showbiz fable. As a child performer, Lotta honed her singing, dancing, and comic abilities in miners' camps and gambling halls, and by the time she was twenty, she was a headline attraction in the country's finest variety and legitimate theatres. Her mother, Mary Ann Crabtree, managed Lotta's career and social life and is arguably rivaled only in her matronly influence by the stage mother of all stage mothers, Gypsy's Mama Rose. Lotta retired from the stage at the height of her fame in 1891, and at the time she was reportedly the highest-paid and most-photographed actress in the United States.

Regrettably, Lotta Crabtree is all but forgotten today except by a handful of theatre historians and aficionados. She left show business just as motion pictures were gaining technical legitimacy, but film musical buffs may think they know her from *Golden*

Girl (1951), the Twentieth Century Fox movie starring Mitzi Gaynor. The biopic plays fast and loose with the factual elements of Lotta's life, but Gaynor's no-holds-barred approach to a song-and-dance number and the character's pluck and determination within this Civil War melodrama make this exactly the kind of role the celebrated soubrette of the gold mines might have played during her heyday. The movie rarely resurfaces, and as Lotta's further descent into obscurity seemed assured, there is reason to rejoice, then, with the reprinting of Constance Rourke's *Troupers of the Gold Coast*.

Rourke's foundational book was first published just four years after Lotta's death and about the same time her will was finally settled (and laying to rest the claims of the staggeringly greedy eighty-seven individuals who had contested the will's charitable bequests, including several people purporting to be her illegitimate children). The work honors the unique talents and career of Lotta Crabtree, but it does much more, as well. *Troupers of the Gold Coast* presents a swirling panoramic view of popular entertainment in the second half of the nineteenth century, reflecting the political and cultural tensions manifested, negotiated, and burlesqued on the national stages in pre- and post-Civil War America. The Yankee, Irish immigrant, Indian, Mormon, and nearly any other national, religious, or ethnic identity one could name were represented for laughs or sympathy in plays and variety acts. Most prominent, however, were the ubiquitous and troubling blackface minstrel acts that dominated the stage for almost a century and the traces of which are still evident today. Indeed, caricaturing race and class distinctions was the great American pastime. In a single performance, for instance, Lotta Crabtree might warble an English ballad in the personage of a cockney waif, execute a spirited and comical Irish jig, and don blackface to sing a "coon song" while accompanying herself on the banjo. As Rourke's impeccable research indicates, performances in variety theatre illuminate the cultural anxieties around national identity, class, and race in the United States of the nineteenth century.

Populating the pages is also an assemblage of theatrical women rebels, whose performances and public personae challenged conceptions of gender and sexuality. Lola Montez (née Eliza Gilbert, later the Countess of Landsfeldt)—Lotta's mentor and early dance teacher—was famous for her "Spider Dance," during which she revealed far more than one presumed acceptable by a lady on the stage. Adah Isaacs Menken—the nude-appearing, breeches-wearing, horse-riding, and cigar-smoking actress and poet— was one of the first individuals to exploit the burgeoning medium of photography and became an international star. Laura Keene, Rowena Granice, and Mrs. John Drew (née Louisa Lane), among several others, were powerful theatre managers, and they defied the domestic constraints and limited economic expectations of women of the era. These women were the industry's pioneers, and the legacies of Lotta Crabtree and her cohorts can be traced through the chronicles of countless women in show business who followed.

Troupers of the Gold Coast remains as relevant today as it was in 1928. Both as a historical document and as a documentary history, Rourke's book reminds us that popular entertainment reveals and shapes moral and social attitudes. In the last decades of the nineteenth century variety acts, minstrel shows, and legitimate plays were, for good *and* ill, part of the lifeblood of the American experience. The kernels of modernism and cultural upheaval were contained within those attractions. The performers brought their shows to the farthest reaches of society, from urban playhouses to country saloons to mining camps. In the process, these fearless troupers, creative geniuses, and savvy celebrities embodied and rehearsed the principles of democracy, and their stories reflect all of the contradictions, vicissitudes, and potential monetary windfall that come with the territory.

—James F. Wilson
Professor of Theatre and English
City University of New York

SALUTATION

IN THE MAIN THE PLEASURES OF WRITING ARE MIXED
with those of solitude, but occasionally a lucky choice of
subject leads to a many-sided collaboration, so that a book
becomes in the end the product of many hands and a
mingling of many enthusiasms. This book is the outcome
of such good fortune. First of all, the past has been a
responsive ally. The men and women who lived in the
midst of that ardent movement known as the gold rush
were stirred as few others have been to put into words the
novelty and force of their experience. Seldom has a compact era had so ample a personal literature.

Personal memoirs have been widely drawn upon for
this narrative: but these are so well known to special
students and so easily accessible to others that it seems
pedantry to name them, and perhaps an indulgence as
well, for they invite a more discursive comment than can
properly belong to these pages. A few, however, may
stand as an index. Among these are that pioneer work of
convivial recollection, Barry and Patten's *Men and Memories of San Francisco in the Spring of '50*, the inimitable
Annals of San Francisco, Lloyd's *Lights and Shades of
San Francisco*, Kenderdine's *A California Tramp*, Mrs.
D. B. Bates's *Incidents on Land and Water, or Four Years*

on the Pacific Coast, and the all but classic memoirs of
the delicate and charming lady who called herself Dame
Shirley and betrayed so genial an appreciation of a rough
life against which she might have been expected to rebel.
Pleasure and an intimate suggestion have come from
Shinn's *Mining Camps,* Old Block's *Sketch-Book* and his
Idle and Industrious Miner, from Asbury Harpending's
Great Diamond Hoax, and that most agreeable compendium, *The Sazerac Lying Club,* with its lavish outlook
upon the untrammeled settlements of Virginia City, Carson City, and other camps in Washoe, whose theatrical
outflowering is part of this narrative.

A passion for the theater ran like a strong and brilliant
coloring through all that animated life, with values still
strikingly illuminated in many open sources. In the files
of contemporary newspapers of San Francisco, Sacramento, Sonora, Grass Valley, Placer and Sierra County,
Shasta, is gathered an abundance of material on actors of
the time, their personal history, their traditions, the plays
in which they appeared, the response of their public.
Such periodicals as the *Golden Era,* the *Pioneer,* the
Californian, the *Dramatic Chronicle,* and *Figaro,* contain
ample sequences of theatrical criticism and commentary;
and the county histories provide many salient outlines of
character and events.

Out of the past have also come old play-bills, miners'

song-books, minstrel and variety songsters, prints, scrap-books, filling in the larger picture with color and detail. A wealth of suggestion appears on the broad hangers as to favorite lyrics, *entr'actes*, and afterpieces, as well as sharp glimpses of personal destiny through the shifting of parts or changes in companies.

Many of these materials are contained in the collections of the California State Library at Sacramento, where the writer found so congenial a collaboration that a large share of the book seems rooted there. To Mr. Milton J. Ferguson, State Librarian, a most agreeable obligation is acknowledged, for an understanding of the difficulties which beset research, for providing conditions for work which approached perfection, and a friendly assistance which has continued through many months. From Miss Mabel R. Gillis, Assistant Librarian, have come constructive suggestions which have taken many important forms. To Miss Eudora Garoutte, Chief of the California Department, the writer owes a debt which can hardly be paid. Her devotion to her chosen field of California history has been a continual stimulus, her scholarship an unfailing resource. Without the newspaper index which is one of the outstanding achievements of her department, much of the work on this book could hardly have been accomplished, or accomplished only with great difficulty. To both Miss Garoutte and her assistant, Miss Caroline

Wenzel, the writer offers the most grateful appreciation for a patient assistance on many questions which have run far afield, and up and down the years.

To Mr. Fred R. Sherman of San Francisco the writer owes a special debt, through the use of his finely balanced and abundant collection of rare California theatrical programs, representing every phase of the life of the California theaters, from the most ambitious classic performances to the wagon shows of the mountains, and a wide and interesting number of minstrel and variety performances. Two of these hangers have been reproduced in this book, by Mr. Sherman's kind permission. In addition, portions of Mr. Sherman's extensive musical collection have been most generously placed at the writer's disposal, including rare sheet-music, old song-books, and variety songsters of early mining days.

To Dr. George D. Lyman of San Francisco, whose large and richly representative collection of rare books on California, pamphlets, manuscript material, programs, and prints, the writer has been permitted to use with great freedom, a large obligation is most cordially acknowledged. Many pieces of material have come to light through Dr. Lyman's collection and by his suggestion.

Another collection, rich in theatrical photographs, rare prints, and programs, which has been levied upon with pleasure and profit for this book is that of Mr. John S. Drum of San Francisco, who has permitted a most ample survey of these materials, and the use of his charming miniature of Lola Montez for illustration. To Mr. J. Harvey McCarthy of Los Angeles most cordial thanks are offered for permission to use in reproduction another rare portrait of Lola Montez.

From Mr. C. K. McClatchy of Sacramento, whose knowledge of theatricals on the Coast reaches into many localities and turns back through many years, the writer has gained a most stimulating range of information, through his own writings on the early theaters, his collection of pictures, and conversation.

Mr. John J. Newbegin of San Francisco has furnished a wealth of suggestion as to the location of new material, and has permitted the use of manuscripts, broadsides, and pictures in his possession. Mr. John Howell has generously allowed the use of portraits and other pictorial matter which have been helpful in making actual both people and places. Mr. Albert Dressler has given the writer access to his files of Sierra County papers, which have proved invaluable in establishing essential links in this narrative.

For the use of manuscript materials, prints, and books, the writer offers tribute to the Society of California Pioneers and to its Curator, Miss Eliza M. Kline, whose kindly assistance has extended far beyond the limits of her duties in the Library of the Society. Appreciation is offered to the Reference Department of the San Francisco Public Library for an extensive coöperation, and likewise to the librarians of the Sutro Collection, the Bancroft Library, the California Historical Society, and the Huntington Library. To Mr. George Barron, Curator of the M. H. de Young Memorial Museum of San Francisco, the writer is under obligation for assistance in using the collection of photographs, scrap-books, and files of county newspapers in the Museum, and by no means least, for as superb a collection of stories, running back to Spanish days in California, as it has been the privilege of the present writer to hear on any subject at any time.

Many stories, many recollections, a wide retrospect of the past through friendly sources have gone into the making of this narrative, which is indeed woven of these around the outline of recorded fact. For this personal and pleasurable research Mr. A. M. Robertson of San Francisco provided the initial key, with conversation about the past which set a tone and level of interest, and the favor of sending the writer to a group of other persons who have a store of knowledge.

This circle has continually widened. Reaching back for three quarters of a century is the memory of Charles Dormon Robinson, whose father, the irrepressible little Dr. Robinson, figures largely in these pages. Indeed, some of young Mr. Robinson's own experiences on the theatrical scene appear. By good fortune this narrative has been enriched by the recollections of Blanche Chapman, a

later member of the famous Chapman family who played
so brilliant a part in early theatrical history in California.
Emelie Melville, of the great stock company at the California Theater in the early seventies, has talked to the
writer out of an ardent memory, as has Clay Greene.
For charming portraits and interesting critical material
on Julia Dean, most grateful acknowledgment is made to
her daughter, Mrs. James Potter Langhorne.

Blanche Bates has generously given the writer spirited
accounts of the life of players in San Francisco and
Washoe, as remembered from stories of her mother, Mrs.
F. M. Bates, during the variegated sixties, when a leading theatrical diversion of the day was to battle with
Maguire. From Ina Coolbrith have come significant memories, offered with humor and wisdom, out of the same
period, when Miss Coolbrith belonged to the group which
included Bret Harte, Charles Stoddard, Mark Twain, and,
during her transient orbit on the Pacific Coast, that
dazzling luminary, Adah Menken.

Ralph Wray, whose personal recollection of the California theaters goes back to the sixties, whose devoted
knowledge begins in '49, who played with Jake Wallace
—trouper with Lotta—and traveled as a minstrel in the
mines with a coach and horses named for the famous
Majiltons, has talked with accurate opulence of these
matters, and as premier jig dancer of his day has enlarged

the writer's knowledge and pleasure by his great repertoire of jigs, reels, breakdowns, step-dances, of the most
finished and intricate order.

Of Lotta—every one knows that except for the most
formal purposes she was never anything but Lotta—many
friendly sources have combined to offer materials from
which might be drawn a personal and theatrical portrait.
To Miss Sophia C. Livesey, Mrs. Oliver Perry Evans,
and Mrs. Charles A. Worden must go the writer's most
cordial appreciation for essential details as to Lotta's
career from the time of her first tour of the California
mining camps as a child. Mr. Thomas Walsh of New
York has provided memories of Lotta in later years, with
a sensitive interpretation of her character and of her comic
art. Among actors who have known Lotta or have played
with her, Kate Mayhew, Julia Wheeler Morrissey, and
Frank Ferguson have given the writer lively remem-
brances of both early years and late, while the writings of
many fellow-actors, of many critical enthusiasts, from
Hutton, Modjeska, and W. H. Crane, to the recent
memoirs of Francis Wilson, have combined to build up an
impression. Prompt-books and script of many of Lotta's
plays have been studied. To these sources have been
joined the many materials on Lotta in the Locke Collection of the New York Public Library, in the collections
of Messmore Kendall and Albert Davis, and the rich
aggregation of programs, photographs, clippings, scrap-

books, and files of theatrical papers in the Harvard
Theater Collection.

As the sources for this book have ranged from one coast
to the other, so the trail of many interests has led, much
as they did for Lotta and the early troupers, from New
York or Boston to San Francisco, and then through the
valleys into the mountains, along the lode from Mariposa
and Sonora to Grass Valley, Nevada City, Rough and
Ready, with many excursions into surrounding regions.
It becomes difficult to mention the contributions which
new friends and old have made at every turn. The writer's
collaborators have grown to a far greater number than
can graciously be named here. To speak of them all, to
touch upon the glimpses of a past era which they have
helped to create, would be to write another book, a personal record, which is perhaps not altogether concealed
within the present volume. The book itself must in part
speak the writer's appreciation. As this tale has been an
outcome of the pleasures of association, so it is offered in
salutation to the many who have helped to create it, in
California and elsewhere, for good remembrance of the
past.

CONTENTS

ILLUSTRATIONS

OF THE

TROUPERS OF THE GOLD COAST
or the rise of LOTTA CRABTREE

I

PORTSMOUTH SQUARE

AROUND THE CORNER FROM THE NEW YORK TRIBUNE
office, on Nassau Street, in the middle forties, stood a
small bookshop in a low two-story building, where books
were piled high in a hit-or-miss fashion, and odd relics
and trinkets littered the shelves or were crowded against
the small-paned, dusty windows. Dickens had paused
there during his first moody visit to America. Many a
wandering Englishman drifted in to turn over odd vol-
umes. The shop had a dim and singular charm, yet its
owner, a tall Lancashire man with an impractical look,
drew from it only a meager living.

John Crabtree enjoyed a more ample conviviality than
that which came with the tinkling of the shop bell or the
muffled questions of visitors as they turned the pages of
old books. The small New York that lay within a stone's
throw of Nassau Street continually drew him forth.
Arched by a broad sky, with houses mixed among the
shops, the little city still had an air of intimacy. The two

rivers seemed close; the rolling heights of Brooklyn crowded upon the eye. In the lower reaches of the town rose a thicket of masts, hemming the seaward view, yet creating the illusion of seaward movement, so that to the sudden glance the real city seemed at the edge of the harbor rather than along Broadway. Leaving his shop untended, Crabtree might often have been seen along the slips, in grogshops, out again as cargoes were unloaded, or down among the slow-moving, little crowds on the Battery. Lancashire men were supposed to be shrewd and thrifty. Crabtree hardly exemplified the tradition. Yet he did not altogether escape it, for that well-marked heritage was concentrated in the small person of Mary Ann, his wife.

Mary Ann Livesey came of sound plain stock, with a special strain. The women of the family were all small, and embodied its strength. Its men tended to be negligible. Years before, in England, her mother had married Samuel Livesey in the face of family opposition, and had borne him a large family. Then—it almost seemed fate— as soon as their three elder sons were old enough to take their places in the world, her husband had set out with them for India, and had never been heard from again. Without resources or education, unaccustomed to make her own way, Mrs. Livesey had come to New York with her three girls and a younger son, and had set up an upholsterer's shop, keeping her children at her side in a matriarchal partnership. Her twin daughters, Mary Ann and Charlotte, small and neat-handed like herself, were her mainstay. The family had soon built up a profitable trade, making satin or damask draperies and holland covers for furniture in some of the mansions uptown. They were lively; they talked as they sewed, and Mary Ann was the most vivacious of them all. A born mimic, with a rich voice, full of laughter, after an errand to one of the great houses she would repeat what every one had said, would impersonate the mistress, the maid at the door, the gaping newsboy at the railing, and describe an interior to the last dignified portrait on the wall. Sometimes her aitches flew in these descriptions, for she was an emphatic young woman.

In her own family it was always a question why she married John Crabtree. She was pretty, with the wide brown eyes and thick bronze hair which ran through her family, but her prettiness was somewhat belied by her firm mouth and the strength of her chin. Perhaps it was Crabtree's pliancy that attracted her. She may have made the marriage from an unerring instinct to gain a province of her own. If she soon learned that the pliant were double and difficult, and that she could never count on Crabtree, as she called him, she said nothing of it, set out as before to her task of sewing covers and curtains, and was livelier than ever. Proffered sympathy, she looked at the intruder with an impervious air. She had a temper; and the effort was seldom made twice.

A child was born to the Crabtrees in the middle forties, who soon died. In 1847 Lotta was born, and quickly grew into a sturdy little girl, small of figure, with hair a brighter red than her mother's, black eyes, a merry face. Mrs. Crabtree was fond of all her children when they were small, when her instinct for governance could be complete; but her two sons born after the family had migrated to California had by comparison only a marginal claim on her affections. It was Lotta whom her mother passionately cherished, the little girl who looked like the Livesey women.

Since the child was to become an actress, and Mrs. Crabtree a manager, she might perhaps have turned from taste or by chance to the shadowy world of the theater. But she could hardly permit herself any considerable indulgence. Sometimes at night with the child Lotta she went around to one of the theaters and watched the crowd enter. Working at her trade as upholsterer, she may have helped contrive properties and obtained a few passes. But here her vaguely aroused interest had to stop. There was a hole in her purse which let many a coin slide into John Crabtree's idle, well-shaped hands, and she had plenty to consider besides amusement. The bookshop was fast becoming a burden, drawing from her pockets more than it yielded. No one with her hard sense could have continued the shop indefinitely, even with the strain of indulgence which she sometimes showed toward her husband's vagaries. Yet what was she to do? Fate intervened, as for so many destinies, in the blind and glittering movement of the gold rush.

In New York, by the autumn of 1848, men in high boots and rough sombreros seemed to spring from the sidewalks. Merchants, ship-builders, sea-captains, were at the Astor House in feverish debate. New York harbor was full of every sort of craft; tiny sloops were being pressed into service for the voyage to Chagres, to Vera Cruz, or around the Horn. It was a blind, mad, sportive movement, full of elegance and fantasy. Young men from New England decked themselves for the journey in pale gray uniforms trimmed with gold and silver braid and lace, carried handsome sabers, and prepared to cross the plains in gayly painted wagons. One company engaged the services of a well-trained band with half a dozen instruments. Others purchased whistles for signaling in case of attack from the Indians, antique crucibles, magical tests for finding gold, and improbable means of extracting it; and as they prepared to leave, as they thronged the wharves or crowded on ships, or converged toward the prairies, they burst into song. The gold rush was a song-singing movement, accompanied by the prime rhythms of *O Susanna!* which sprang from negro airs and had become a favorite with traveling minstrels. The rich and festive tune became a classic, and was soon surrounded by a whole lexicon of other lively melodies.

The mounting hundreds—soon to be thousands—on the way to California chorused in a single protesting voice that they did not propose to remain there. For duty's sake they meant only to seize enough of the golden profusion to make themselves comfortable for the rest of their days; then they would return to the East, and civilization. Yet there was a strange look of permanence in their preparations. Along with whistles and crucibles they took plows, harrows, farming tools, machinery for harness shops, for pistol and knife factories. They purchased an abundance of seeds for agriculture, even flower seeds. Nothing seemed to halt their plans or progress, not tales of hardship or of disappointment or even of death.

Out by sea and over the plains went the thickening, hastening procession. The ships on the Pacific from Panama were often so closely packed that men went insane with intense discomfort, and had to be lashed to the rigging. Now on the journey across the plains entire parties were not wiped out as they had been a few years earlier; but as these later bands traveled over the old Spanish trail through the Mohave, across Death Valley to the San Joaquin, or by way of the Humboldt River—still the River of Death, its banks a burying-ground—the slighter members drooped and died. When a caravan dipped at last into the lovely American Valley, that green and fertile cup, watered by the Feather River, seemed a dream of paradise: but the women of the company were burnt copper color, their hair and eyes were lusterless, their movements without animation, and the remembrance of the print of death—most often the death of their young children—lay heavily upon them.

Dismal books on California came out by the dozen, and a sheaf of songs—

"I've been to California, and I haven't got a dime,
  I've lost my health, my strength, my hope, and I have
    lost my time,
  I've only got a spade and pick and if I felt quite brave,
  I'd use the two of them 'ere things to scoop me out a
    grave. . . ."

But these songs were sung in an animated falsetto, laughter greeted the darkest prophecies. The outgoing ships still were crowded, the stream of wagons from the Mississippi almost unbroken. Was it only for gold, that glittering mirage which overspread the whole horizon? Or for wild adventure? Or release into the unknown, in that distant country which seemed another continent, another world? One might have supposed that large numbers of men were glad to be rid of civilization and the East.

In this exodus the Crabtrees were caught at last. John Crabtree was born to cry "Westward ho!" In the vague-

ness of that shout was entrancement. Before him now lay
boundless possibilities of fortune without effort, and
chances to roam. The only wonder was that he had not
joined in the first blind departure. Mrs. Crabtree's pru-
dence had been the deterrent; but she too was persuaded
to a belief in golden fortunes, and he finally was off, early
in 1852. "Nothing would do but Crabtree must leave New
York to dig gold in California," she said, and added
briefly, "He never got any."

At least Crabtree became a vague standard-bearer for
the family. In the spring of the following year his wife
followed, taking the route over the Isthmus. Her decision to go West had the look of luck. Poor as she was,
Mrs. Crabtree chose the most prosperous way to travel,
by steamer, on one of those "luxurious white steamers
. . . floating like clouds . . . some of them as large as
two thousand tons." With the tiny roguish Lotta at her
side, by the upright bearing of her own small figure, she
attracted favorable comment on the ship; and there was
plenty to see and to enjoy, from the crowded companionship of the journey across the Isthmus to the fresh voyage
north from Panama. It was the high year for clipper-
ships—the *Jenny Lind*, *Fly Away*, *Snap Dragon*, *Sweepstakes*, *Mystery*, *Morning Star*, which had followed in the
wake of the famous *Flying Cloud*—

"She's a flash clipper ship, and bound for to go,
  Good-by, fare you well, good-by, fare you well!"

The great race between the *Sword Fish of* New York and the *Flying Fish* of Boston had already taken place, with fabulous wagers along the Atlantic seaboard and at San Francisco. Other races hardly less spectacular had followed, some of them impromptu, as one feather-light ship crossed the bows of another. For days at a time the ocean would be sprinkled over with white ships. Whalers could be seen far out on the Pacific. The sound of chanteys rose in the mild distance.

Slowly the coast range emerged, pale gold in winter, now brilliantly green with springing wild oats. As the *Oregon* passed through the Narrows into the rim of low bare hills—gray, blue, gold, purple—clippers glided by on the outward voyage to China and India for return cargoes. River steamers were riding down from Sacramento—

"A Yankee ship comes down the river,
Blow, boys, blow!"

Small craft plied the bay on the way to half-hidden creeks and inlets. Clustered around the steep little city in a western crescent seemed to be assembled all the shipping of the world. Bright flags flew of many nations. On the precipitous sandy cliff of Telegraph Hill waved the legendary black arm announcing the arrival of a steamer. The sound of chanteys rose loud and clear: *O, my Sally!* and *The Banks of the Sacramento,* sung like *Salem City* to a minstrel melody.

Long Wharf looked like a narrow watery village, carelessly planked, with crowded shops and stalls, hackney carriages driving at full tilt, sailors clambering from boat-stairs, men hastening up and down the steep street which led into the city. All San Francisco seemed linked to the bay. Cargoes of teas, silks, shawls, were being lightered into the rear of warehouses on a lower street. Ships beached and embedded on made ground along the curve of shore had been turned into shops and houses, as if rosy old sea-captains should put on tile hats and high stock collars, and sit down, jingling their compasses.

Everything was movement, to and from the wharves, up and down the streets, with furious winds blowing through gaps between the hills, carrying clouds of sand. The fate which had burned the city half a dozen times in rapid succession and had impelled its rebuilding while the old ashes were still hot seemed to stir like a tangible thing within its scattered boundaries.

Far up the irregular channels of the street little frame houses might be seen, with scallops of wooden trimming like coarse lace along their eaves, which all but waved in the wind. Iron houses perched on sandy slopes. Many-colored tents still flapped above the town.

Into the dense and jostling crowd on the wharf Mrs. Crabtree peered in vain. Crabtree was not in sight. She was met by English friends with whom she was to stay for a brief time, and learned that her husband had last been seen in a little town in the high Sierras; and there was no message. Her dismay must have gone deep, but she took the news with equanimity. Perhaps it was not wholly unexpected. Who could count on Crabtree? In any event Mrs. Crabtree had learned to live with her anxieties. She was besides one of those fortunate people who have a permanent alliance with the outside world. To the end of her days she could tell what she saw in the next half hour.

As her little party drove up the steep planking toward the Square they passed dark shops with miners' implements stacked outside. Gold dust gleamed in a jeweler's window. There was an English inn with a green door, flower-boxes, a landlady who might have come lately from Sussex. With a sudden lurch they climbed: the western side of Montgomery Street lay half a dozen feet higher than the eastern. Up and up the city rose abruptly, by planked roads, equally by black quagmires.

They turned into Portsmouth Square, and the whole blazing life of the new San Francisco lay before them. If the gold rush had begun with fantasy, here caprice came into full bloom. Around the steep enclosure of the Square milled an unbroken procession which seemed bent on some preposterous rendezvous of play or masquerade. Gray uniforms and gold lace might have been torn to tatters on the journey out, but the lads who had worn them could now assume sweeping sombreros and black velvet cloaks. Young Americans galloped through the crowd in all the old splendor of the native Californian, in serapes, glittering spurs, brilliantly decorated saddles. From risky side streets dashed brightly painted carriages lined with rich silks, drawn by pairs of fine horses. Red-shirted miners on foot slung their pistols with an air of grandeur. Gamblers proclaimed their calling by a cluster of feathers or a squirrel's tail in their hats, and by snowy white shirts with large diamond studs or massive gold breastpins.

Every appearance was highly keyed or brightly colored. Knots of Germans, Italians, Frenchmen, seemed more strongly racial than in the land of their birth. A mixed populace—Americans of every lineage, British soldiers of fortune, Kanakas, Abyssinians, negro slaves brought to work in the mines, Chinese women, delicate and bold—all were flinging off on their own errands, yet all seemed bound together by some novel freemasonry.

"They were a wild, perverse race, the San Franciscans of those days," said one who loved them well. "Life in California impressed new features on old characters, as a fresh mintage on antiquated coins," said another seeking to explain the change. "The men whose practical maxim" —in the Atlantic States—"is a bird in the hand is worth two in the bush, will here throw all his birds into the bushes, seemingly for the mere excitement of catching them again."

Nearly all of them were young; they were posturing, perverse, humorous, desperate, a single extravagant whole; and Portsmouth Square was their sporting-ground. Rising tier by tier on its four sides were substantial buildings, some of stone faced in China, some of painted plaster with ample balconies and finely wrought railings. Most of these were gaming houses, showing glimpses of ruddy interiors, giving out through open windows shouts of laughter, the sound of flutes and fiddles, the quick smiles of women who dealt cards or turned the wheel. Gambling was the great public diversion—gambling and the theater. On a corner of the Square stood the handsome building which had lately been the Jenny Lind, built by Tom Maguire and now sold to the city as City Hall, the third theater of its name on the site, each rising after a disastrous fire. A little below on Washington Street was the lively little San Francisco, still farther down, on Sansome, the large new American Theatre. Not far up the hill was the Adelphi. A half dozen smaller houses of entertainment were scattered near by. The gambling saloons often became theaters for a night. The Bella Union on the Square, the most notorious of them all, had already played an essential part in the theatrical history of San Francisco.

Gambling and theatricals were inextricably interwoven in the city and in the mines; and both were accompanied by a richly flowing bowl. Every gambling house had a bar. Every theater had a bar at its entrance, even the decorous

Adelphi, with its classic lintel and look of reticence.

Prim young Mrs. Crabtree, how did she take all this bold pleasure? With aversion and with relish. She never approved of it, yet she liked the sharp variety and highly splashed color. And at the moment, as she drove through the crowd, she became aware of a friendly promise. Children were still an uncommon sight in San Francisco. Lotta was gay, with her bright black eyes and red hair. Hands were outstretched as they passed. They were traversing a scene which was to become endlessly familiar, passing characters with whose lives theirs were to be closely intermingled. Even in a procession which ran boldly to the picturesque, certain figures stood out by reason of a highly trained effectiveness, some tilt of the head or motion of the hand or singularity of costume. These were theater people. San Francisco was full of actors. They had come from the show-boats of the Mississippi, from the small theaters of Mobile, New Orleans, Galveston, Nashville, Cincinnati, from New York—actors, opera singers, musicians of all orders, vaudeville and circus performers, bands and bandmasters. They had converged from the ends of the earth, from Australia and even China, from England and France, Italy and Sweden. They had come by steamer or small sailing craft around the Horn or even across the plains on foot. One company had traveled from St. Louis in prairie schooners with friendly Sioux as companions for part of the distance.

Actors were still coming, confident of fortune, aware that the life of the stage was flourishing in California with extraordinary vigor and abundance. Young Edwin Booth, who had played *Hamlet* for the first time a few nights before, might have been seen riding down to rehearsal on a high white horse—hardly more than a boy, dark and pensive. Mrs. Judah, a towering personality in any assemblage, who carried something of the strangeness of her history in her look and bearing, may have walked past. As the Crabtrees crossed the Square, Tom Maguire perhaps emerged from a bright doorway. He was always smoothly appearing, always on view, quiet and somnambulistic, hat well on one side, long cigar at an opposite angle, the mark of the gambler in every aspect of his resplendent appearance—Maguire who could neither read nor write, the cab-driver who had come from nowhere, turned gambler, had begun gambling in theaters, and who now held the fate of many an actor or company in his hand.

Nothing could have seemed less likely than that small Lotta Crabtree would mingle with the crowd of actors in the Square as one of their number. Many of these older players were seasoned. Some of them came from established families of actors with a long schooling on the stage. The Crabtrees lacked even a shred of theatrical tradition. Yet after only a brief interval Lotta was to begin the long and ample adventures by which she became a prime favorite in California and later throughout the country, dancing, singing, the most popular soubrette of the day, or more truly a comedian, setting new fashions on the stage, splintering old ones, enclosing in her own small person a whole lively page of American theatrical history. For a time she seemed only a prankish small imp who was always near by at high moments. If she never quite pulled aside the curtain for older actors she was usually no great distance away, peering around the corner as they came into view or dancing with hoydenish handsprings on an obscure near-by stage. From a distance the lively little thing seemed to pick up many an unexpected clew to new theatricals, creating meanwhile an art of her own. No other player was so deeply rooted in the local scene, with so wide a later career. She was to outlive every one of the actors now gathered in California, to surpass them all in fortune, and to emerge from the stress of years as a charming, slightly enigmatic personality.

II

MAGUIRE

A MARKED DRIFT OF FORTUNE WAS IN THE HANDS OF young Mary Ann Crabtree. Certain persons have a faculty for crowding upon events, for entering fertile fields at timely moments. Mrs. Crabtree possessed this, though she was to encounter plenty of adversity. Even as she drove out through deep cuts to the worn and gulleyed road which led to the home of her friends near the Presidio a transient luck seemed her portion. The house was spacious, with a wide garden and willow-trees: here she could remain with Lotta until Crabtree was discovered. But the special favor came from the larger circumstance of time and place.

In a hort four years the life of the stage in California had become as well marked and as full of passionate change as that of a full-bodied individual; and this brief history was a matter of common lore. In San Francisco, with its air of a universal holiday, news was the readiest commodity. A population which only a year or two before had slept in tents or endured the bunks of crowded lodging houses had learned to spend their days in the streets or places of entertainment, flocking and talking together.

Everybody had news—news of the theaters. Perhaps few cities have gained so rich a theatrical tradition in so brief a space.

Like every newcomer Mrs. Crabtree heard numberless stories of theatricals, which she hoarded because thrift was her nature, and because she was uncertain what the future in this strange new country might bring. Struggling for a foothold, she grasped at every straw. Like every one else she had traveled to California with the hope of new fortunes; she wanted change. But if she listened to glittering episodes, with her resistant skepticism she also picked up every scrap which came her way as to the tragedy or ill luck which had befallen troupers on the Coast. Gradually, in spite of herself, she was drawn toward that many-colored life which seemed so firmly rooted in the Square. She liked that chequered, bizarre existence, even while she felt that she did not belong there. Slender as was her purse, she went to the theaters. Who indeed stayed away?

Was it for herself that vague plans were taking shape —or for Lotta? At the moment the child seemed infinitely remote from anything which had to do with theatricals. When at a near-by school she had been led to a platform in her little starched dress to sing *Annie Laurie* for a celebration she had broken down, cried bitterly, and had to be taken home; the closely crowding faces in the small room were too much for her. It was only among people whom she knew well or in a large throng, as in the dense and

changing groups on the Square, that the child became herself again. Lotta was unabashed in a large crowd; and
Mrs. Crabtree heard many tales of children who were
dancing and singing in the mines or even occasionally in
San Francisco. Who were they? What did the miners like?
What had happened in that crowded history? A little
eagerly, perhaps inexorably, she turned toward the whole
bright spectacle of California theatricals of the past and
present, asking, guessing, judging, piecing the tale together for purposes of her own. She could scarcely step
into the streets without seeing or hearing something which
had built up that many-colored existence.

Throughout the city like a singing undertone still remained traces of those pleasurable lost years of Spanish
California which had seemed to provide an instant background for theatricals, when *rancheros* played the guitar
under ladies' windows while their horses stepped in
measure to the melody, when the fandango was an elaborate ritual with choruses bordering on the operatic. Spanish
airs could still be heard in the streets of San Francisco.
Every native Californian played the guitar. Fandango
houses—rude indeed—were scattered through the city and
through the mountains. Bull-fights at the Mission, another
relic of earlier days, were announced by a tall negro bell-
ringer in a blue coat and white beaver hat who walked
through the streets. A light jingle, a merry melody were
everywhere. Gamblers carried little bells with which to

ring for drinks or cards. Musical entertainers roamed about. One of them, strangely elegant, was an Englishman in a light brown hat with a high crown and narrow brim, a frilled shirt and elaborate cravat, who played an instrument known as the pipes of Pan, or antique cymbals, or a triangle, or an accordion, or a bass-drum, according to his pleasure, and at intervals toured the mines.

If not wholly theatrical these sounds and appearances were in friendly alliance with the theater. Interludes of singing and dancing were popular on every stage, as if the cult of an earlier California had joined with that of the roaring, song-singing newcomers. But the amazing circumstance was the spontaneous eagerness with which the Americans had turned to the drama itself. Even the soldiers of Stevenson's regiment who had arrived before the discovery of gold, who had come for the soberest reasons, not only as soldiers, to hold the country, but as colonizers to settle there, had begun almost at once to give plays. They had been chosen for their useful trades; they were blacksmiths, carpenters, mechanics. They had come from little towns in the East where theaters were almost unknown. Yet they had hardly arrived when they had set about the business of theatricals. At Monterey in the spring of 1848 the wing of a long adobe house was fitted up for them as a theater, with a pit, a little stage, and a wooden drop curtain which was lifted and lowered like the lid of a box. Here they produced stout old English farces and even Shakespeare.

At Sonoma in the Valley of the Moon another company of the regiment turned to theatricals at about the same time, and played for four months in a miniature theater. The unexpected enthusiasm sprang up in San Francisco. A few young stragglers of fortune united in the spring of 1848 to give plays. Another band met in the autumn for the same purpose at the dubious Shades Tavern. The building of a theater was discussed even when the town was only a scattered village of tents and tiny wooden houses.

A stout red-faced little Englishman with a great mop of curls and a proud bearing gave the first public entertainment in San Francisco, on an evening of June, 1849, in a crowded little room on the Square before a crowd of newly arrived gold-seekers. This was Steve Massett, who called himself Jeems Pipes of Pipesville, a rolling stone who had maneuvered himself around the world and was to continue on the endless journey, though with long and repeated sojourns in California. Massett was a composer of graceful melodies and lyrics which became highly popular throughout the country during the fifties and sixties. He could turn into a rousing and accomplished auctioneer when necessity pinched, or an editor, or even a persuasive peddler of harmoniums. For his first performance he sang some tender tunes of his own in a fine baritone, and burlesqued a well-known singer of the day in an equally fine falsetto.

Burlesque was perhaps Massett's greatest accomplishment. He reeled off half a dozen daring imitations of Yankee character, ending with a broad picture of a New England town meeting in which he played seven parts. He was irresistibly funny: and the audience, largely composed of Yankees, roared with laughter. Massett had in fact opened the door wide for California theatricals. Burlesque of all kinds was to flourish there, and Yankee imitations became prime favorites.

A band of minstrels appeared in San Francisco in '49, but their stay was brief. One of the bones was killed in a brawl at the Bella Union, and the unlucky troupe fled to the Sandwich Islands.

A circus—Rowe's—opened with a company of nine at a new amphitheater which seated over a thousand persons, where lady circus-riders leapt safely from one broad wooden saddle to another on slowly galloping steeds, and the horse Adonis struck classical attitudes. For a few weeks the place was packed.

Then at a sudden stroke in '49 San Francisco was empty. Ships still drove in numbers through the Narrows, but many of these sailed up the river to Sacramento, and hundreds more brought to anchor in the bay were deserted before their cargoes could be unloaded. The only

captain who succeeded in forcing his men to the final task
was an actor who had master's papers and a gift for rant.
He terrorized his crew. But they too were soon off to
Sacramento.

Dripping in the winter rain, caught in a forest of masts
and arching greenery, Sacramento in the late autumn of
'49 looked like some transient city built for pleasure over
a lagoon, now reluctantly turned to human habitation.
Camp-fires smoldered in thickets of live-oaks on the
plain. Huddled in tents or small cabins were hundreds of
miserable human beings who had endured the hard over-
land journey and were now impoverished, and suffering
with fever and ague. In the spring Sacramento had been
a cluster of four houses; now ten thousand people were
encamped there and more were constantly drifting in.
Men came down from the mines laden with gold which
they spent as freely as though the golden stream would
flow on forever. A young lad snatched a jew's-harp which
had cost less than a penny from Steve Massett's auction
tent, flung down a nugget of gold worth eight dollars,
and ran off playing tunes. A Swiss organ girl was accumu-
lating a neat fortune playing in Sacramento and in the
mines. The watery little city, so dreary in appearance,
grew riotous with entertainment.

Here, in October, '49, the first complete theatrical performance in California was given in the new Eagle Theatre, a small affair of canvas walls with a roof of sheet

iron upon which the rain beat a smart tattoo. At its door
stood the long-remembered Round Tent, the most popular and magnificent gambling tent of the moment, lit by
torches and decorated by dubious pictures. The stifling
interior of the theater boasted a dress circle and a parquette, so-called; the stage had a drop-curtain. Foliage
of dark red, Hildebrand in a sky-blue mantle, the knight
in purple, two specters in dirty tent canvas holding
spermaceti candles in their hands, the lady of the piece
shouting, "No! I'd rather take a basilisk and wrap his
cold fangs around me than be clasped in the hembraces
of a 'artless robber," or wailing to the knight, "Me 'ope—
me only 'ope!"— these made a dramatic effort which was
received by the crowded miners with a loud shouting
laughter which all but shattered the players.

Other romantic melodramas were valiantly offered on
successive nights, with the same wild reception from the
audience. When the curtain went down monte decks were
produced. As the rainy season advanced and the river overflowed its banks, gradually creeping into the theater, the
band had to be placed behind the parquette. That space
was finally flooded, and the miners sat on the railing,
clapping their hands with broad gestures which sent un-
wary neighbors into the water. Knives and pistols flourished and hysteria reigned, as men were drawn together
before grotesque scenes after the isolation of the mines.

In a few weeks the flood was at its full, Sacramento was

dotted with sail-boats, and the Eagle Theatre Company was washed down the river to San Francisco, where they opened at a quickly contrived little hall in *The Wife*. This play, with its tale of the constancy of a woman, seldom failed to bring tears to the eyes of a company of argonauts in spite of the stilted confusion of its action and its battered blank verse. But harried by laughter in Sacramento and by the flood, the company was perhaps not equal to emotional efforts. They were coldly received; and to cap disaster their treasurer gambled away their earnings at cards.

Once more the enterprising Rowe came forward, this time with actors who had recently arrived from Australia, and began a series of ambitious performances at his amphitheater which even included *Othello*. But in the midst of the sawdust his plays grew irresistibly lighter and lighter. Presently in *Rob Roy* the whole circus company crowded in, hostlers and horses and all. Then the actors quarreled with the circus people; and the circus triumphed. Evidently their entertainment failed to please, for before long Rowe had left for the Cannibal Islands where he was courteously received by the inhabitants, who viewed the feats of the lady riders and the classical attitudes of the horse Adonis with grave curiosity, and permitted the band to leave for Australia intact.

Down the rivers to San Francisco the miners came in increasing numbers through 1850, hungry for further

amusement, ready to scatter gold dust. There was still a
dearth of competent players. After all, ready as they had
been to see the promise of theatricals on the Pacific, actors
had moved far less quickly than gold-diggers. At this
juncture, on a comparatively empty stage in San Francisco,
an angular little figure emerged who had notions of his
own as to the kind of dramatics demanded in the town.
This was Dr. Robinson—Yankee Robinson, one of several Robinsons who adopted the designation in this period,
though none of the others possessed so striking a character. No doubt Mrs. Crabtree learned much of him, for
he was still a dominant figure in the San Francisco of
1853. She would have done well to listen closely to all
she heard, for Dr. Robinson possessed secrets of the California stage adapted for her later use, and she was to
meet him in more than one important encounter.

Briskly enough, on January 1, 1849, Dr. Robinson had
arrived in San Francisco, a New Englander, born in
Maine, a wandering trouper, playwright, manager, who
had had an alliance with Barnum. In a little side street he
contrived a small audience hall when colors were so scarce
that he was obliged to use mustard and curry instead of
chrome yellow to paint the backdrop. Since other substi-
tutes were missing, the single thick and garish tone prevailed. When this theater was destroyed in the great fire
which all but leveled San Francisco in May, 1850, he had
built Robinson and Evrard's Dramatic Museum, on Cali-

fornia Street, a cozy place, seating about two hundred persons. There he began giving entertainments with a strong local flavor. Since actors were scarce he engaged a group of willing amateurs, trained them, and made the most of their local connections in songs or parts.

His first play, *Seeing the Elephant,* was an elastic sketch which had first been given in New York to ridicule the gold rush. To see the elephant, in the great popular phrase of the time, was to go to California expecting good luck at every turn, and to be monstrously tripped up and deceived by fortune. All the miners' hard experiences, rough travel, cold, hunger, encountering bears or bandits, finding poor claims—these were "seeing the elephant." The phrase was everywhere. Elephants appeared on letter paper, were painted on miners' cabins, adorned that manifesto of morals known as *The Miner's Ten Commandments.* The little play had been given once before in San Francisco, but without adaptation to the local scene. Dr. Robinson laid the main portion of the story in the city, gave it many an adroit amusing twist, and burlesqued the part of the distraught and beaten Yankee, Seth Slopes, who was the hero of the piece.

From the opening night the Dramatic Museum was crowded. Miners pushed and edged and fairly fought their way to see this glittering mirror of themselves, and to see Dr. Robinson. With a knack for drawing character, a rich dialect, and inexhaustible high spirits, he seemed to act for his own amusement. His song and pantomime called *The Old Umbrella* became so popular that if he failed to give it without the tangible old ragged umbrella a clamor rose from the house. His wailing, drawling *Used-up Miner* was sung all through the mines—

"Oh, I ha'n't got no home, nor nothin' else, I s'pose,
  Misfortune seems to follow me wherever I goes;
  I come to California with a heart both stout and bold
  And I've been up to the diggin's there to get some lumps
    of gold—

"Oh, I'm a used-up man, a perfect used-up man,
  And if ever I get home again, I'll stay there if I can—

"I lives way down in Maine, where I heard about the
    diggin's,
  So I shipped aboard a darned old barque commanded by
    Joe Higgins,
  I sold my little farm, and from wife and children parted,
  And off to California sailed, and left 'em broken-
    hearted—

"And here's a used-up man . . ."

Further and further he dipped into the local scene, and introduced well-known California characters in rhyme. With a sharp satire he portrayed nearly every political figure and nicked a few tricksters.

Seeing the Elephant became a merry-go-round, taking on a fresh load of characters and songs every trip. The faster it whirled the better the miners liked it. They shouted questions with a wit of their own; and Dr. Robinson was swift in repartee. They bawled forth the choruses of the better-known songs. From the moment of their arrival the argonauts had liked song and satire: here they had both, with a picture of themselves, of which they never grew tired. For the first time a genuine popularity was created on the stage in California, with that ready give-and-take between the audience and the actor which need not always be turned into words but whose spirit is essential in the making of a theater. The Dramatic Museum prospered so richly that Dr. Robinson was enabled to engage professional actors as they appeared, and to vary his offerings with occasional Spanish dancers. Presently he built himself a comfortable New England house on the high bare eminence of Telegraph Hill, where the black arm announced the arrival of steamers, where he could command a view of the bay, and look down upon the rapidly growing city.

This conspicuous enterprise came to the leisurely attention of Tom Maguire, who decided that the next good risk in San Francisco would be a handsome theater, and who perhaps wished to give rein to a fantasy of his own. It was always a question, then and afterward, how Maguire, whose ignorance of the stage was abysmal, contrived his long career as a theatrical promoter. He was credited with an occult power in judging character, and may have possessed it. Certainly he had the lavish touch. The Jenny Lind, upstairs over his gambling saloon, the Parker House on the Square, was adorned with richly gilded proscenium boxes, a gilded ceiling, and panels of deep rose; its stage was wide, with a painted drop-curtain. As for an audience, in fancy Maguire took a long stride forward. Instead of the paltry two hundred at the Dramatic Museum, he envisioned two thousand, and his theater was built proportionately.

Legend surrounds the Jenny Lind, legend of a charming humor. Jenny Lind herself never went to California, though many persons there in the fifties were to declare to their dying day that they had seen and heard her, and were able to describe precisely how she looked (she was usually dark) and what she wore (most often checked silk) and would name the theaters in which she sang. By 1850 her name was everywhere, floating out from the eastern states through Barnum's magical energy. A clipper ship in the California trade was named the *Jenny Lind*. Gambling houses all along the Coast, a Swedish band, a camp in the Sierras, the old adobe theater at Monterey, and a steamer, took the name. Maguire seems to have chosen it because it was in the air, and perhaps because he had a lasting obsession about music, though no one was ever able to prove that he was musical.

Maguire spared nothing for the Jenny Lind in the way of opulent settings, and gave over the theater to James Stark, a tried actor, a fine reader, something of a scholar, who had recently come across the plains, and who now produced in rapid succession full versions of *Macbeth*, *Hamlet, Lear, Richelieu, Much Ado, The Rivals, Pizarro*, with a sheaf of English comedies, and a changing number of light afterpieces. Maguire had made a successful throw, with his grandiose visions. The Jenny Lind was continually crowded. Miners still packed the Dramatic Museum, but they also swarmed from the gambling saloons and cheap fandango houses to see *Hamlet* and *Lear*. Apparently craving elegance, in a raw little town where there were still few women, where men were bitterly uncomfortable in makeshift lodgings, where horses were sometimes drowned in mud, this audience received suave comedies of manners with unbounded enthusiasm.

Theatricals came to a full and sudden bloom in San Francisco. Farces, pantomimes, minstrels, might now be seen at half a dozen gambling saloons. Masquerades had a great vogue. In a rough little hall called the Adelphi, upstairs on the south side of the Square, the first operatic performances were given. On a tiny stage, lit by sperm oil lamps, with dim scenery and before a small audience, a little French and Italian troupe sang arias from a few operas, and soon ventured into performances of *La Som-*

nambula, Norma, and *Ernani,* even though they had no chorus.

But the odds had seemed against any lasting endeavor in the theater. Early in May, 1851, San Francisco was again swept by another disastrous fire, in which the Jenny Lind, the Dramatic Museum, the tiny Adelphi, and other less well-established houses were destroyed. Maguire at once rebuilt the Jenny Lind. The new theater had a shadowy existence of just nine days, when this too was burned to the ground. By October he had again rebuilt his theater on a scale unprecedented in California, and perhaps elsewhere in the country. The third Jenny Lind was large and handsome, of cut stone with simple arches; its spacious interior was gorgeous in red and gold. If the drop-curtain showed too many scenes painted in too gorgeous a confusion, after all, it was lifted to display a stage of generous size and excellent equipment.

For its opening *All That Glitters Is Not Gold* was offered, which had had its first production in New York only six months earlier, and was to be performed over and over again in California, in many a small theater in the mines as well as in Sacramento and San Francisco, chosen perhaps for the bright suggestiveness of its title, yet maintaining its place because of something solid and worthy in its theme and construction. The new company at the Jenny Lind was hardly less important than the play. Maguire had acquired some of the luster belonging to the

name of Booth, in young Junius Brutus. Within June
Booth, as he was soon affectionately called, the ancient
madness burned only meagerly, but he was a good-
humored manager and actor who was to remain in California for many years; he had brought with him a well-
rounded group of players; and the new productions at the
Jenny Lind were ambitious. A brilliant new pantomime
was given, *Cherry and Fair Star; or, The Green Bird, the
Dancing Waters, and the Singing Tree.* Difficult Shakespearean performances were achieved, as of *Henry IV,*
with a score of new Yankee plays and English comedies.

Theater building and management in San Francisco had
begun on a wide, enduring scale. The small and pretty new
Adelphi was finished. The Jenny Lind had hardly opened
its doors when the American Theater began its career,
elaborate with Corinthian pillars supporting the first tier
of boxes. Rich draperies and handsome lamps adorned
the interior; there were a pit, a parquette, a gallery, a
gilded dome which seemed to shed its rays over painted
clouds and to transmit radiance to the scene below.

These early years were full of episodes that drifted into
legend. On the opening night the American, which stood
on a quagmire, settled palpably with its audience. The
poetical salutation was spoken by Mrs. Stark, who possessed a passionate sense of melodrama. "Could we to-
night the eternal slumbers break," she boomed—

"Of Avon's bard, and bid the dreamer wake,
   The astonish'd muse would bid the Poet turn,
   And sleep again beneath the honored urn. . . ."

This little quip, whose intention Mrs. Stark may never have perceived, had perhaps been contrived by Dr. Robinson, who had moved swiftly from the ashes of his Museum to the Adelphi, and then to the American. The lines seemed an index of that unblurred view which seemed to belong to the mixed and changing public. With all the gorgeous appurtenances, with all the ambitious plays, there were plenty of theater-goers who realized that some of these new ventures failed to fulfill the highest theatrical traditions, that the parts were often over-acted, and productions put together with more energy than art. But there was warmth in the audience as well as humor, something palpable and genial that all but floated in the air.

The little doctor was always being called before the curtain by the shout, "Tell us a story, tell us a story!" His local songs were sung between the acts. In all directions his sallies let a fresh wind into the theater. That spirit of burlesque which had been abroad from the beginning might have been concentrated in his own small person, puncturing pretensions, lighting dull places. But Dr. Robinson came to grief through Mrs. Stark.

On the evening of a performance of *The Stranger* at

the American, Mrs. Robinson, who disapproved of
theatricals, awakened her small son Charles, dressed him
in a red plush suit, and went to the theater, having promised to introduce him at the proper moment into the scene
where the distracted heroine calls for her child. The
journey down Telegraph Hill was murky, the rear
entrance to the theater dark. Carrying Charles, she picked
her way across the planking over the mire on the ground
floor, climbed a ladder, and reached the level of the stage
just as the child's cue was spoken. Perhaps he was insuf-
ficiently rehearsed; certainly he was sleepy, stiff, and hot.
His mother gave him a vigorous push. There was a dazzle
of lights, and Mrs. Stark, a very large woman in a black
dress, rapidly moved across the stage toward him on her
knees with arms outstretched, shouting that she wanted her
child. Charles was terrified; and as it happened he was a
small expressive pattern of his father. With a comely oath
he stamped his foot, shouted at Mrs. Stark, stood his
ground, and ruined the scene.

Afterwards Mrs. Stark accused Mrs. Robinson of having accomplished the catastrophe by design. The Starks
left the company and went back to the Jenny Lind. In
rejoinder a rousing benefit performance was given at the
American for Mrs. Robinson by a grateful company. But
this was Dr. Robinson's final fling at that theater. He
lacked a sufficient number of competent actors. He closed
with a performance of his own, at the end of which he

introduced Charles in the historic red suit piping up the song *Nary a Red, Nary a Red,* with a play on words in which all miners delighted, and a frank intimation of his father's plight. This—and the child's ease—broke up the performance. There was a supper afterward at the Occidental with beaten biscuits and champagne, with Charles on the table and the whole town present. With his usual ingenuity Dr. Robinson had changed something which bordered on catastrophe into a gay finale. He clasped hands with his audience, left a following to which he could return when he chose, and mounted the peak of Telegraph Hill, where he was said to be writing a play.

Maguire as usual held the proverbial card. The Chapmans were coming to the Jenny Lind. Not George Chapman, his wife, Miss Mary and Miss Josephine, willing, agreeable actors who had been in and out of his and other theaters for a year or more, but the more famous members of the same family, Caroline Chapman, and her brother William, who were to dominate the California stage through a bright heyday.

Almost any one who had followed their career might have predicted that the Chapmans would go to California. Their rivals declared that they were gypsies. Close and secretive, they had a habit of finger communication, and used a slurred, rapid, manufactured language of their own even in the greenroom, which set them apart from other actors. One of their ancestors had played the original Beggar in *The Beggar's Opera.* A prolific English family, they clung together. Under the patriarchal William Chapman, who had played in Covent Garden in the reign of Mrs. Siddons, they had come to America in the late twenties, and had soon begun to wander, moving from the eastern cities into little towns of the middle states. Then, about 1830, from a love of hazards and of the open air, and from a preference for their own society, they invented the first show-boat, and floated up and down the Mississippi.

Those were years when troupers were often driven out of the smaller towns of the Middle West, but the Chapmans could sail away when hostilities threatened, or put on plays for their own amusement when the audiences were lacking. Their family had become large enough through marriages and growing offspring to make a company without assistance. They worked tirelessly at a large repertoire, played classic tragedy, danced, sang, and acted in blackface, and at lazy intervals fished.

> "Oh, won't you—oh, won't you
> Go along with me
> Away down the river
> Through Kentucky—"

Bearing its flag with the single word "Theatre," with a comfortable little house forward, and the plain little hall with wooden benches, muslin curtains, and a tiny stage aft, the show-boat of the Chapmans had plied up and down the Mississippi for ten years, between 1830 and 1840, when this idyllic existence was broken by the death of the elder William Chapman. The family had scattered; Caroline and her brother, who had grown up on the show-boat, had made their way to New York, where Caroline rose to a charming eminence at Burton's. She was never beautiful; in repose off stage she seemed awkward; but in the leisurely life on the Mississippi and through the ardent teaching of her family she had gained a wide expressive range. Once in a part her plain features took on something like radiance, her dark eyes flashed, her lanky figure melted into grace. With contagious vivacity she could play low comedy, burlesque, sing mock Italian bravura, and impersonate Mrs. Bracegirdle in *The Tragedy Queen* with something of the Covent Garden splendor. Her brother William, always a quieter talent, built up a solid reputation for close character portrayal, though he too had a strain of comedy which veered toward burlesque.

At the Jenny Lind the Chapmans poured forth a profusion of plays, many of which had not yet been seen there, Shakespeare, English comedies old and new, the latest farcical successes in New York, and produced these in the midst of a richness of setting for which Maguire seems to have enjoyed the mere dispersal of gold slugs. The pair came forth with the grand musical spectacle of *Clari, Maid of Milan*, then with a burst of exuberant production which ran rapidly to extravaganza. They gave *The Naiad Queen,* and followed with the still more lavish *Fair One with the Golden Locks* and the spectacular *Green Bushes.* Then to prove that their horn of plenty held every conceivable pleasure, they had turned easily to a rich and solid *Dombey and Son.*

Playing as out of boundless high spirits, they matched the surcharged energy of a lavish audience, and showed a light but arrogant sense of rivalry. Their musical extravaganzas had perhaps been induced by the great popularity of Biscaccianti, who was now singing in the city. They raced with the Bakers, intelligent and interesting new players at the Adelphi. Willful and formidable, the Chapmans set a new high level for the California stage. As powerful characters of the stage they seemed to bring others like them in their train. After their arrival a bold procession of insurgent personalities began to move among the theaters of San Francisco.

Mrs. Judah came, impressing her public as much by her character and history as by her acting. As a young woman during the early forties she had played in New Orleans and in the South, had reaped a golden harvest in Tallahassee, and had set sail with her husband and two children for an engagement in Havana. The ship was wrecked, her husband was drowned. For four days and nights she had floated with her children in the storm, lashed to a spar, and the children had perished of starva-

tion and exposure before her eyes. She was saved at last
by a passing fisherboat. With a stalwart mind as well as a
constitution of extraordinary vigor, she soon appeared
again on the stage. Even as a girl she had liked old
women's parts; now she chose to play nothing else. After
a long season at the Boston Museum she had come to San
Francisco to stay. For thirty years she was to support every
important star, and to overshadow many of them. Sooner
or later nearly every one of the actors gathering in the
city was to feel both her iron and her kindness, the perva-
sive tragedy of her life and her humor.

Within a few weeks after her arrival the elder Booth
walked upon the scene, tramping down from the steamer
with an old carpet-bag in his hand, rough as any figure on
the wharf, yet with something heroic in his carriage, and a
rude deliberate survey of his fellow-men that was part
of his habitual gaze. He had looked before on strange settings in out of the way places, as he had traveled in the
South and through the middle states like any utility
trouper during the forties, offering Racine in French at
New Orleans and *Venice Preserved* at Mobile, often
absorbed in fantasies which had nothing to do with the
stage. In Ohio he had once sought out clergyman after
clergyman, trying to arrange a fitting burial for a pigeon
which he had found slaughtered out of a dense flock of
pigeons. Given to mysterious disappearances and a changing fancy, that wild genius had on the stage the intensest

concentration at high moments. The more troubling the outward circumstances, the more complete seemed his ironic grasp of the bitter parts he chose to play. Now he had come toward the end, and perhaps he knew it. Yet, as a child remembered, he "strode off like a drum-major" into the streets of San Francisco, with his son Edwin, a slender lad hardly nineteen, at his side.

The Jenny Lind, which Maguire had quietly sold to the city, was retained for Booth's performances. The Chapmans, Junius Booth and his wife, Edwin in a few productions, with a few others made up the company. Booth opened at the end of July, 1852, in *The Iron Chest;* and though the season had grown dull the excitement which followed was little short of breathless.

There was tragedy in the spectacle, not only because Booth was failing. He was playing now in the midst of forces which were breaking the high conventions of the stage which had been his own. Perhaps he had seen the signs before he left the East. Here, in a new and untrammeled theater, they were abundant. Caroline Chapman played with a natural grasp of the essentials of character within which her strange native passion could overflow, but she had cast away nearly everything of fixed tradition she had ever known. The elder Booth played within a ritual, essentially simple, by which every touch of action or of business had long since been prearranged. If the mold seemed rigid, there was beauty—or might be

—in final revelations of character. Within that deep pattern a wild and transcendent life might burn, as if by the
renouncement of small individualisms an inner understanding could be made complete.

Booth played with his old magnificence, shattering the
appearance of age. Even through the grandiose structure
of a play like *The Iron Chest*, that single and dynamic
tortured power which was his broke into fire. In *Othello,
Hamlet, Macbeth, Richard III, A New Way to Pay Old
Debts,* he played apparently with all his accustomed passion, with a subtle and sudden revelation of agony, anger,
guilt, remorse. Of all emotions perhaps remorse was that
which Booth still revealed with most compulsion, in a
vein of blackest tragedy. And that volatile San Francisco
public, so recently pleased with extravaganza, so easily
slipping into indifference, listened to Booth and watched
as though he was the only figure on the stage. Deeply
shaken, the same audience came night after night. The
Jenny Lind was packed to the doors during the brief two
weeks of his engagement.

At Sacramento Booth's fortunes were reversed. His
audience from the first was unresponsive, and soon
dwindled; he lost the profits of the earlier engagement.
In that city, close to the mines, concentrating the perils and
rapid fortunes of the new adventure on the Coast more
completely than any other place, where the sharpest con-
trasts still reigned, Booth's anguished sounding of tragedy

was perhaps not only unwelcome but unbearable. Suicides were frequent there, as elsewhere in the gold regions. Men were constantly drifting in who had suffered disappointment, loneliness, cold, hunger, beyond the limit of human endurance. If they survived, if in the warmth of saloons and gambling halls or by some chance contact they gained a new foothold, they hardly looked for comfort in tragic portrayals. Booth returned to San Francisco for a brief engagement of five days at the Adelphi, for another tense response, when every nook and corner of the little theater was crowded, playing for his final appearance *The Merchant of Venice*, and departing a few days later for New Orleans alone.

He seemed to have had no thought of a career for Edwin. The boy had appeared on the stage only two or three times in the East. In Sacramento he came to his father's dressing-room garbed in black for the part of Jaffier, and Booth told him brusquely that he looked like Hamlet, and ought to take the part for a benefit if he ever had one. Yet when the manager of the theater had wished to include Edwin on the bill, his father had forbidden this, saying that his son was a good banjo player —as if that were all—and might be announced for a solo between the acts.

In the roughly charted careers of the troupers who had come to the Coast was a hint of more than one personal crisis. In the many changes, the rise and fall of

obscure actors, might be traced the plain outlines of ambition, failure, and despair. One of the Australian actresses
had committed suicide after an unsuccessful season. Others
had been reduced to small entertainments in gambling
saloons. Yet among all the personal situations which were
common knowledge, few perhaps comprised one so dark
or so subtle as that in which young Edwin Booth now
found himself. He had been his father's guardian since his
early boyhood; and that tie had had many a fantastic re-
enforcement. From the wings he had watched the elder
Booth play his essential parts of desperate sin and remorse
again and again. In *The Iron Chest,* which Booth had
offered repeatedly in California, the oblique relationship
was materialized with Edwin as young Wilford, who had
sought to learn the secret locked in the mysterious chest
which Booth as Mortimer tried to conceal, thrusting the
boy out into a hostile world, even attempting his life in
passionate defense. The theme of the play was now repeated. The elder Booth had at last severed the long close
bond of personal guardianship, either for Edwin's sake,
or because he preferred to be unaccompanied on his last
errands.

The wrench went deep; and the world which confronted Edwin and even his more practiced brother Junius
in the autumn of 1852 was hostile enough. Neither had an
opening. Maguire had transferred the Jenny Lind to the
city. The hardy Chapmans were off to the mines, the first

really accomplished actors to make the tour. With one less theater in the field the Bakers had begun a season at the small Adelphi distinguished by the solidity and finish of their offerings, which already included a notable succession of Shakespearean productions and of Dickens plays. Mrs. Judah had joined their company. At the American Theatre a brilliant attraction of another sort had crowded forward. Kate Hayes, the willowy Swan of Erin, had arrived, fresh from triumphs at Covent Garden and a successful season in the East, accompanied by a competent manager who had enlisted the rousing loyalty of the local firemen. The effect of the Kate Hayes concerts was resplendent, and all but obliterated the memory of Biscaccianti, who was now singing in the interior. Presently the Swan herself had moved on to Sacramento, where another tumultuous welcome awaited her. For her first concert the choice of seats, purchased at auction for a fabulous price, was given by the Sutter Rifles to Captain Sutter. The stout, affable, disillusioned old man had made a conspicuous entry with a detachment of officers to the sound of thundering applause, and was seated with ceremony in the front row on an opulent and spacious green plush sofa.

Young Junius Booth at last succeeded in obtaining the management of a Sacramento theater, but he was hardly installed there when the city was leveled by the great fire of November, 1852. With an obscure traveling company

Edwin went up the valley, pausing here and there, playing the banjo at unknown camps, giving whatever entertainment he could contrive, arriving at last in Nevada
City. The winter of 1852 was bitter in the mountains, with
torrential rains and snows; there was a shortage of food,
particularly in the north. The town of Nevada, perched
astride a cañon and a creek, crowning a hill torn by flumes
and honeycombed by tunnels, seemed a frozen ruin. The
whole hill was rich with gold—gold of the finest quality
and most beautiful color—but the exhilaration which
covered the headlong assault upon claims in fair weather
was gone. In a town which was a cluster of dingy canvas
tents and log cabins with a few staring white houses,
money was lacking as well as food.

Young Booth could hardly have given enough dash to
his performances to have enlivened a crew of discouraged
miners. He ventured one of his father's great parts, Iago,
for the first time, but made little impression. He strummed
the banjo. Then actual famine set in. The theater was
closed, and credit refused the company. In the midst of
cold and hunger Booth learned of his father's death alone
on a Mississippi riverboat. At evening of a bitter day a
fellow-actor brought him a letter. Edwin read the look
on his companion's face, and asked the question, "Spear,
is my father dead?" Beset by catastrophe, the whole company walked down steep and scarcely broken roads
through snow to Marysville, where they disbanded; and

Edwin, still on foot, made his way into the slough of the
Sacramento Valley, and then to San Francisco.

Sad enough, young Booth plunged at once into a brilliant and astonishing scene. By one of those sudden
changes which were both the life and the terror of the
stage in California, the whole theatrical situation had taken
on a new pattern. Maguire had by no means retired from
theatrical control when he had sold the Jenny Lind. He
had only shifted his ground. Within a few months he had
built the San Francisco Hall on Washington Street, a
"neat little temple," as one admirer called it, a "heart-
delighting, side-splitting little *bijou.*" The San Francisco
was dedicated to mirth; and the most spontaneous talent
of the stage was gathered there.

The Chapmans were back from a riotous tour in the
southern mines, where their gyspy temperament had had
full play. They too had suffered from cold and from
perpetual rains as they had ridden into the San Joaquin
Valley; the pinch of winter, less sharp toward the south,
was nevertheless in the air. As they left the coaches in the
lower foothills they had been obliged to proceed on mules
or horseback by narrow trails to the camps on distant
placers and gulches. Bandits prowled through these
regions; this was the wide haunt of the fabled Murietta.
But perhaps the Chapmans liked the flick of danger. They
had hardly missed a camp. At Campo Seco a new little
theater of boards and canvas had just been opened, with

the inevitable bar in front. They had played in cloth and paper houses, in bars, in flimsy hotels, and were received with an enthusiasm which bordered on tumult and was colored by passionate affection. They played at Columbia, one of the largest camps in the mountains, which had grown up almost overnight and was indeed a city, sprawled within a brilliant green curve of upland covered with wild oats, cut and gashed by mines. Here in the fandango houses celebrations had grown so tempestuous that a venturesome local legislation had attempted a curb. The beating of drums and playing of trombones had been prohibited. But this effort at restraint had signally failed. When the Chapmans arrived, late in 1852, midwinter festivities in Columbia were at their height.

The theater in which they played had been built by that wild actor who had terrorized a crew into unloading his ship in San Francisco bay. Perhaps he joined them for a brief season. Their whole tour had been an affair of chance combinations with strolling actors or with amateurs who had taken to the boards in the winter months. The Chapmans were a careless pair, caring little enough with whom they played. They struck a high arrogant key; theirs was the rapid tempo of the life about them. They could have kept these alone in readings from the stage. The miners grew hysterical with pleasure, and at the end of the first performance flung buckskin purses loaded with gold over the candles until the floor of the stage was carpeted. In a mob they followed the Chapmans to and from the theater at every performance, and on succeeding nights showered silver coins upon them in such profusion that there was a shortage in the region until spring. The mob grew. When the Chapmans moved on to Sonora for the grand opening of the new Phoenix Theatre on New Year's Eve a horde of miners a thousand strong formed their escort. In Sonora, Caroline Chapman spoke an opening poetical address on the small new stage in the rear of a saloon. At the last, as if in tribute to a vivid character which had already become manifest in that rough mining village, with an elaborate high humor the Chapmans produced *She Stoops to Conquer.*

No doubt Caroline Chapman and her brother William extracted a final pleasure from that tour. In the freedom of the mining camps they could be as willful as they liked, as extravagant in their interpretations, as companionable with each other. They had returned to San Francisco with a fresh and abounding energy, and had at once been installed at Maguire's new theater, where they began pouring out a profusion of new and quickly changing performances. Caroline Chapman was now "Our Caroline." She seemed "to perform as much for her own amusement as for that of her audience . . . to relish every point, to revel in her own sprightliness," to act with "a dashing but very graceful offhandedness with which at the first bound she leaps clean out of the reach of criticism." Junius Booth had been installed as manager with William Chapman; and Dr. Robinson, his long rivalry with Maguire ended, had resumed his favorite rôle of personal entertainer. He sang between the acts—his *Old Umbrella* now ran to forty-six verses—put on brief local sketches as after-pieces, and even acted in full-length plays.

It was in the midst of this highly strung company that the stray sad young Edwin Booth found himself after his bitter journey early in 1853. Within a few days he was playing the lead in *The American Fireman.* Presently he came out as the negro dandy in a blackface version of *Box and Cox,* and plunged into the popular pastime of burlesquing local celebrities. Higher and higher ran the fun at the San Francisco. Comedies of all kinds, high and low, English comedies of manners and local burlesques, Shakespearean productions and musical extravaganzas followed in rapid succession. A continual freshness and variety pervaded the theater. Indeed, the complaint was heard that too many plays were produced, that the performances were not sufficiently finished or the lines well learned. Dr. Robinson was mildly censured for too daring a wit. But the performances remained unfailingly popular; and Caroline Chapman could hardly touch a play without giving it at least a sparkling surface.

Thus San Francisco Hall was the prime center of entertainment in the city during the spring of 1853, when

Mrs. Crabtree arrived with a tiny unschooled star in her train. She liked what she saw at this theater, the high burlesques, impersonations, lively songs, the brisk comedies. Caroline Chapman perhaps left an impression as to the daring means as well as the possible charm of the feminine comedian. Mrs. Crabtree was indulging a hearty sense of comedy; hers was a temperament in which humor ran deep. No one who lacked humor could have taken Crabtree's absence so calmly, unless she was stolid—and that Mary Ann Crabtree never was. It was a sense of fun, something young and girlish and irresponsible in spite of her essential firmness and her cares, which drew her to the parti-colored life in the Square.

Out of the whole scene she was choosing what best suited her. From the past she wove her own conclusions. A figure like the elder Booth would never have attracted her except as sheer character. It was his strangeness, his madness and gusto and his tragic end which she remembered, as a story: she never would have been drawn to his acting. Young Edwin Booth seemed to her only a pale lad with a melancholy air who took comic parts badly. If he had just played *Hamlet* for the first time this was a circumstance which would have concerned her very little. Mary Ann Crabtree was uninterested in Hamlets. Tragedy was not her vein. As she looked back, it was comedy which she saw always bubbling up in those early hurry-skurry efforts in the theater, from the days of Massett and the first minstrels and the first circus to these merry nights at the little San Francisco Hall. Perhaps she was right in her conclusions. Perhaps the sense of sheer fun—struggling, hysterical, triumphant, unfettered—had been dominant in all that ambitious turmoil of acting.

At least for herself she settled the question once and for all. She was dogmatic. What she knew was a finished affair. In later years she argued about comedy. "It's life," she said, firmly if a little obscurely. Yet, as she looked about, with her sharp and unflinching gaze, her own entrance into the world of the theater must have seemed preposterous. Before her was a powerful gathering of highly trained actors, bound together into what seemed an impregnable whole. The group at the San Francisco was deeply entrenched, with connections which ran far afield through the Chapman Family, as George Chapman, his wife, younger sisters, and children were now called. They frequently dashed into the city to join the company at the San Francisco and to play at other theaters, as did another group of related Robinsons now rising into view, among them the child Sue, who was being talked about by the incoming miners as a promising child actress and dancer who had been seen in the interior.

Even in the way in which they lived these actors seemed to dominate the city. Around Dr. Robinson's house at the top of Telegraph Hill almost all of them had gathered in little frame houses strung together in an irregular

cluster, with crooked brick walks between and steps leading
from level to level. If Mrs. Robinson looked down on
actors and most particularly on actresses, she was none the
less an exemplary housekeeper with a gift for hospitality.
Her house was always full of players on their way in and
out of the city. There were merry dinners at the Chapmans' on Sunday, and gay suppers after the play, when
the party of actors would climb the precipice by lantern-
light. William Chapman—or Uncle Billy, as he was
called by the growing flock of children—rode down into
the city and back again over steep crags which he seemed
deliberately to choose for his route in a two-wheeled cart
drawn by a mule. There was a horse which belonged to all
the colony, that would drink champagne from a silver
cake basket, and then float away with its rider down the
further side of the hill to North Beach and out to the
Presidio. No place in the city was livelier or more inviting
than that bare cliff where these actors lived. Picnic parties
came to those precarious ledges. A Chinese theater had
been built on the slope, with gongs and strange music.
The black arm announcing the arrival of the steamer
would wave from that eminence, and townspeople would
troop up to look over the bay.

The only one of the group who lived apart was young
Edwin Booth, who had a small house of his own near the
Mission Dolores, dubbing himself "comedian and
ranchero" in the new city directory. The place had a

blurred and dusty charm, out a winding way among sand hills and chaparral, near a cluster of Spanish adobes. Here were many traces of the earlier Spanish life, with a bull and bear arena near the church, a race track, a road-house called the Nightingale and another called the Willows. But even at this distance Booth was not isolated from theater people. He lived with an old actor known for character parts. In the same colony was the redoubtable Massett, Jeems Pipes of Pipesville, always returning from foreign regions.

Scattered throughout the city actors of all ranks, minstrels, opera singers, French vaudeville performers, utility troupers, many musicians, were woven into its substantial color. Many a minor troupe was penetrating the interior. Theaters were being built at Marysville and Grass Valley, and as far up into the mountains as Downieville. Sacramento had two handsome new theaters. Stockton had had a charming small playhouse, with cushioned seats, private boxes, damask curtains. If this had gone the way of most new buildings in California, in a sudden puff of smoke and flame, another was now being projected. At Mokelumne Hill, a riotous camp near rich gulches which had been successfully worked since the winter of '49, where sharpers and desperadoes of all nations had gathered, and men had been killed by bowie knives flung at fifty feet, amateur theatricals had begun to flourish almost as soon as a settlement was made, and had continued to thrive, with the miners attempting such emotional plays as *The Wife* in true rendering or in burlesque, producing original plays, and laboring to construct elaborate settings and mechanical stage devices.

In no other area of the country had the theater come into such unchastened, free and abundant life. Elsewhere the theater had always suffered from repression, except perhaps in a few scattered cities of the South. On this new frontier nothing was repressed, either plays, actors, or the audience. Men quarreled over renderings, and protested when lines were cut. Acting versions of plays often changed hands among the miners for more than their weight in gold. If burlesque and extravaganza prevailed, every new experiment in the theater was welcomed. Recondite plays like *The Critic* had been produced; and the rewards offered to favorite players remained lavish, taking the form of a rain of nuggets in the camps and often in San Francisco, with the cosmopolitan addition of diadems and watches, golden flowers and jeweled brooches.

Even as young Mrs. Crabtree tried to make decisions there were two more conspicuous arrivals who gave to that insurgent life a further brilliancy and scale. Catherine Sinclair came, bearing with her the import of her recent suit for divorce against Edwin Forrest, of her witty and charming sudden appearances on the stage immediately afterward in New York, and her intention to find a place for herself in theatricals on the Pacific Coast. She at once joined the players at San Francisco Hall.

The other new arrival was Lola Montez, the Countess of Landsfeldt, the Limerick Countess, the Spanish dancer, born Eliza Gilbert in Ireland, who came with dash and drums and all the paraphernalia of romance, her slender figure carrying the semblance of great history.

In the midst of this final dazzling display Mrs. Crabtree may have wished to remain. The town was briskly talking. But a letter had reached her from the mountains: Crabtree had been in the high Sierras, where he did not precisely say, nor was his errand there explained. It had to do with gold, but he did not discuss his luck. In fact he had a new project under way, something which he did not name, though obviously from the excitement in his scrawl he considered it a bonanza. With Lotta his wife was to come at once to Grass Valley.

Mary Ann Crabtree was a little skeptical, a little pleased. She tied up her conclusions about the theaters as firmly in her mind as though they had been a little parcel of goods which she could put in her reticule. After all she hoped she might not have to use them. Perhaps fortune would come, without great effort, in that sudden dazzling fashion that seemed usual enough in California. Mrs. Crabtree had her moments of the common madness. She started at once with Lotta up the Sacramento River on the way to Grass Valley, a little town perched midway up the mountains to the north.

III

COUNTESS OF LANDSFELDT

Up the sacramento in the late spring went our travelers. Trim white steamers plied the river and jockeyed for place within blue deep graceful bends, joining in races past drooping willow-trees. Shouts, laughter, bells, rang out; convoys of light sailing craft drifted by. Music, bountiful good food, clean linen, decks crowded with men and an increasing number of women hopefully seeking new fortunes—all augured a positive luxury of luck.

A shadowy city lit by flares and torches appeared as Mrs. Crabtree landed in Sacramento with Lotta late at night. By dawn they were ready to travel again, looking for places in a stage-coach in the midst of dancing lanterns, shouts, the pawing and whinnying of horses. Drawn up abreast in a narrow street, the coaches were crowded together, some of them primitive affairs with only an awning for covering, some handsome painted Concord stages with curved bodies and high wheels. The last strap of harness was hardly buckled when the horses were off to run at full tilt through the city and out over the great level plain with nothing to halt them, no hedges, no ditches, scarcely a road. In the gray blackness live oaks made a feathery gloom. Here and there were the embers of night fires or a sudden red blaze which showed contorted bows dipping almost to the earth. Within a delicate bright canopy of tiny leaves moved dark figures stirring for a journey as in the midst of a huge rosy lantern. A few wayfarers could be seen already on foot or on horseback moving with the pale shadow of the plain.

With the quick pouring flood of sunlight the whole floor of the valley was spread wide. Like trees in spacious orchards the green live oaks seemed laden with heavy invisible fruit. Ruddy larks sprang from the earth. Pearly white convolvulus opened its spreading wheels. Snowy elder was in bloom, wild roses, blackberry vines, clematis, and virgin's bower. Hazy to the right and before them as they drove were the high Sierras, aquamarine blown over by pale mist. After a few hours the road began to ascend, grew steeper. Out over airy suspension bridges, past miners washing gold in little streams, brushing near small camps and stopping, on up, the coach climbed at last to the village of Grass Valley.

The whole region might have belonged to quite another land from that in which young Edwin Booth had spent so disastrous a season only a few months before. The shallow slopes between Grass Valley and Nevada City were now opulently green, the tossed earth in the deep gullies looked rich and fertile. Clear snow-fed streams poured through the valley. Dark pines rose thin and pointed on

the higher hills. In the fresh light even remote peaks
seemed accessible—places to wander—their cleft cañons
dark and cool with oak and manzanita. To the newcomer,
to young Mary Ann Crabtree, all this outspread prospect
was full of promise. Fertility was everywhere, gold lay
almost within the grasp, in the sifted red earth, in the
pale translucence of broken quartz. Men trooped by on
foot or on horseback with all the signs of conquest and
possession. Gorges were being spanned, tunnels dug, shafts
sunk, water lifted from deep cañons over ridges and
foothills and wooden flumes built by the thousand yards.

Alas! John Crabtree had no aptitude for the herculean
labor of disemboweling the earth. Nor was he one of
those lucky fellows of whom current tales were full, who
could roll off cliffs in their sleep, and unhurt, without
turning over, begin to dig out nuggets from a rich pocket
with a jack-knife. Men like Crabtree invariably left a
claim just before a strike was made. Wandering about in
the high Sierras he had accumulated nothing but hope;
and his project, advanced so enthusiastically in the letter
sent to San Francisco, hardly held out the promise of fortune, though perhaps it embodied a lasting fancy of his
own. Crabtree was convivial. He proposed to keep a
boarding-house. Two of the richest merchants in Grass
Valley were in need of a home, he explained; others
would quickly come; their house—their little inn—their
hotel—would be crowded. In the mines every one spent

money readily. There would be chances for good profits, for partnerships in gold-digging, lucky tips—of course!

Mixing and baking were a poor end for all that bright-hued travel to the golden coast. Heretofore Mrs. Crabtree had had nothing to do with a kitchen. In New York the thrifty Livesey family had given their energies to the up-holstery business and had kept a servant; after Mary Ann's marriage the two households had joined at table. Mrs. Crabtree ran the boarding-house capably, but in a spirit of rebellion. She firmly considered new possibilities. Gold—how was she to obtain it? For herself, for Lotta—perhaps even for Crabtree, whose share in the new enter-prise of the boarding-house grew lighter and lighter and finally vanished.

As hot summer descended on the valley, as Crabtree roamed farther afield prospecting, his wife talked with men and the few women who had been longest in the mountains. No one with a roof overhead or food for the next meal could have grown discouraged. If fortune was not at hand it was always just beyond. Some months earlier a whole regiment of gold diggers had crowded northward in ships expecting to find miles of beach on the Pacific so rich in gold that the sand need hardly be washed, and pans could be used as shovels. They had come back again, ready for another fantastic journey. The higher Sierras were said to be made of gold—if only human in-genuity could devise a means to tear away the rocky crust.

EDWIN BOOTH. 1852

PORTSMOUTH SQUARE

Drawn from an old photograph by W. J. Aylward

There were lakes of gold, lost to view and hard to find. The color of gold was always to be had by small effort.

Exhilaration—possession—movement—gold, seldom to keep but always to spend—were everywhere. Over a high winding road which looked as though it were on a rim of spacious color, with rifts of copper pink in the hills beyond deep valleys, purple and lavender to the north, lay the rousing camp of Rough and Ready, which had earned its name by a history of wild dances held to the whistling tune of bullets riddling the ceilings, and a first swaggering stress upon an undomesticated existence. Plenty of the first tempest remained there; the place was full of gambling halls and saloons; bull and bear fights were still a diversion. Saucy ballads like *Hangtown Gals* were heard perhaps more freely than *Belle Brandon* and *Sweet Annie of the Vale*; and racing had begun on a tiny track circled in a hollow below the town.

Here gold poured in from rich gulches and was lavishly gambled away; and the bright parade of digging and entertainment had become embedded in a wider and more stable scene. Ranches now spread within fertile dips of valley; wheat fields were ripening, orchards clung to the hillsides. Some of the lower foothills were covered with vineyards. If rough fandangos were common enough, there were also balls to which women came from neighboring ranches wearing low-shouldered silk dresses with rippling long full skirts. Round about, drawn by the loadstone of wealth, a many-sided community was growing up, pleasure-loving, possessive of tangible good things of the earth. Everywhere good food became a cult. Not many months earlier at French Corral, where more than a thousand miners toiled in a deep and narrow cañon not far from Grass Valley, a grand ball had been given with arbors built for the outdoor repast, and tables loaded with turkeys, roast pigs, jellies, East India preserves, sweetmeats, ice cream, with flowers gathered many miles up the mountains near snow-level, and ice brought down for the frozen delicacies. If the camp had recently gone up in flames it was being swiftly rebuilt as though for another summer fête.

Peddlers traveled through these camps carrying enormous packs of velvet, silk, workaday calico, smart broadcloth coats, laces, sealing-wax, yellow-backed novels, sometimes copies of the novels of Dickens, even the plays of Shakespeare, and a hundred trinkets, all strapped into a pack as solid as iron and worn on their backs, unless they had grown prosperous enough to ride mules.

With little money to spend, Mrs. Crabtree could only hold aloof from such attractions: but Grass Valley was soon in the throes of an excitement in which she could easily join. One day in midsummer 1853 Lola Montez came wheeling up to the town in the coach from Marysville with her new husband, Patrick Purdy Hull, looked about, laughed, said she liked the place, and would re-

main there. Rumor, flying fast as to everything which concerned her in the few weeks she had spent in California,
had said that she was bound to find a mountain retreat.
She bought a house a few steps away from the Crabtrees,
down a rough mountain trail, a one-story cottage set back
from the road behind white palings, with French windows,
a wide veranda, and a deep doorway which seemed made
for a more formal dwelling. Within, the simple rooms
had the same look, with slightly arched ceilings, a broad
hall, and a passage-way at the back which divided the
living quarters from the rest of the house. Here she unpacked her trunks filled with spoils from Europe, and soon
made the little yard bright with a profusion of rose-trees,
with flowers and shrubs from the mountains; she planted
cactus there, whose grotesque beauty she liked. Presently
she bought two bear cubs from a mountaineer and began
to train them. Then one day she drove down to Marysville
with Hull, and after a violent quarrel returned without
him. She resumed the name of Countess Landsfeldt, and
faced the village.

Legend enveloped that strong-fibered personality.
Every one knew her story. San Francisco was full of men
of foreign birth who had learned of her in the larger cities
of Europe. Even in Grass Valley, with its considerable
French colony, were plenty of people who could report
her escapades. When she realized that her first appearance
in Paris as a dancer was a failure she had flung her slipper

into one of the boxes; soon afterward she had walked across the flower-beds of Prince Henry of Reuss, and had been expelled from his kingdom. Every one knew of her notorious alliances, and was aware that her bold and lovely eyes had scanned the entire European horizon until they discovered a biddable king, and that in Munich as the Countess of Landsfeldt, in a house as exquisite as a shell, she had cast her lot with revolution. She was now often flippant about its origin and results; but undoubtedly she loved the center of any storm as some minds love quietude. In Munich she had stepped forth to brave the elements, facing four hostile student corps alone in the streets, drinking champagne in the window when her house was stormed, and at last, when she was driven from Bavaria by the ruler she had influenced, snapping her fingers at his tale that she was a witch visited by a huge black bird, and marrying a snub-nosed young officer in England whose elderly aunt promptly got out a warrant against her for bigamy.

Shaking off her marriages as easily as she did the circumstance of her Irish birth, she had sailed to America in 1851, had been received with a fanfare suitable for a famous revolutionist, and perhaps had laughed at the joke. Certainly the cities in which she had appeared, New York, Philadelphia, Boston, took her too seriously, hoping for an epic in her autobiographical play, *Lola Montez in Bavaria*. Since she was announced as the celebrated Spanish dancer, they had expected a rival of Elssler or Taglioni. But the play was a crude affair, her dancing only vivacious; she had failed in the East, had gone on to New Orleans, and then to San Francisco, to appear without a favorable introduction before audiences which were already schooled and critical, and to be received as a noted character— notorious rather, as she herself said, "for notorious I have always been, and never famous." She offered a puzzle, and she knew it. She might have traveled halfway around the earth, reaching the end of her rope for the amusement of a mystery.

Even in appearance Lola Montez assumed many guises. Most often she has been described as having black hair and black eyes; but her hair, which curled almost child-ishly back from her face, was bronze with dark shadows, her eyes were blue. She was called a "tigress," "a modern Amazon," and was said to have the wit of a pot-house, with the carriage of a duchess: yet she could romp with children and look like one of them. She could also take on the aspect of a blue-stocking, offering the contents of her amazing memory with a pedantic air. She always scorned the furbelows of the period, and off stage dressed soberly in black, with a white rolling collar. She was often said to be the daughter of Lord Byron, and perhaps in-vented the notion. What was she truly? A little weath-ered photograph taken while she was in San Francisco re-veals her as almost severely intellectual, with fearless eyes showing humor, and a witty curve at the corner of her lips. She was habited as plainly as a nun.

In San Francisco she had shaken out her little handful of plays with her dances, including the famous spider dance, while excitement grew breathless: public interest lay hardly at all in either her dancing or her acting but in her character, which was perhaps what she wanted. She was declared to be "a very *comet* of her sex; and we watch her course with the same emotions that we follow the brilliant movements of that erratic body flying through space, alone, unguided, reckless, and undestined." She was considered a child who "thinks that her own nature teaches as correct a rule of conduct as traditions or old customs, which for her have no authority." She was compared to Mirabeau. Her dancing shocked many of the trained theater-goers of the town, but they had their answer. "Lola is singular, but it is her right." They argued about her volubly in verse, in editorials, in the columns of the dramatic critics. They insisted that her auto-biographical play failed to do her justice. "The play represents Lola as a coquettish, wayward, reckless woman. . . . We shall cherish our ideal image," they declared, and gallantly persisted in regarding her as a romantic, historical figure.

Then the powerful band of troupers at the San Francisco Theatre had drawn up their guns. When Lola gave *Maritana,* taking three parts, Caroline Chapman produced a hardy little burlesque called *The Actress of All Work* and took seven. Again Lola came forth with her auto-biographical play, *Lola Montez in Bavaria;* and the Chapmans produced a short extravaganza with the same title which had had a success in New York. Striving for recognition, Lola produced *Charlotte Corday*, and thus insisted upon the serious rôle of revolutionist, danced two spider dances instead of one, and followed with a firemen's benefit at which she gave selections from all her plays. In tumultuous enthusiasm, as she shook the india rubber spiders from her skirts, the firemen cast their helmets on the stage, showered her with bouquets, and demanded a speech, which—remembering that she was Spanish—she gave with a slight foreign accent. She was soon toasted in the town, entertained by such lavish hosts as Sam Brannan, and audaciously strolled into a gambling saloon to play tenpins.

With relentless precision the burlesque *Lola Montez* had been repeated by the Chapmans. The critics railed at the troupe at the San Francisco. Lola asked Dr. Robinson for the reason behind this shattering fun. For a few days after her arrival she had stayed at his house on the peak of Telegraph Hill; and the austere Mrs. Robinson had even helped her make spiders of rubber and whalebone and cork. Dr. Robinson was right enough in replying that burlesque was often a compliment, always an advertisement, and here a native custom: but it may be a question whether he explained precisely what he had up his sleeve at the moment. He had written a full length burlesque on Lola's appearance in San Francisco, a local play, crowded with personal innuendo, bearing the cryptic title *Who's Got the Countess?* This was soon produced at the San Francisco. Building up her travesty on a stormy scene at one of Lola's rehearsals, Caroline Chapman took the leading rôle of Mula, with a superlative enhancement of the quality of arrogance and a wealth of comic by-play. She was fluent, she was confident, and controlled. "If she were to play the devil we have no doubt she would be greeted with storms of applause," brusquely declared one of Lola's most enthusiastic admirers.

Protests were heard on every side; yet the little San Francisco Theatre was crowded at every performance. The daring play was always new. Miss Chapman obstinately stamped, coquetted, and credibly impersonated the Countess, raced through the spider dance with not a touch of its boldness understressed, transforming this indeed into a ridiculous and fanciful ballet called *Spy-Dear!* Gradually Dr. Robinson built up the piece until it included the whole cast at the American Theatre—where Lola had been playing—the manager, the critics, even the audience, not forgetting the prompter, whose part he took himself, and turned into a sharp and glittering weapon of satire against Lola as an actress who never knew her lines.

Lola was routed, not by the public, though San Francisco laughed, but by the versatile and accomplished Miss Chapman, heading a highly charged troupe which had been banded together for months, and by the irrepressible little doctor. After all, the situation had been simple enough. On the stage Lola Montez had thrown down a highly personal challenge, and this had been briskly picked up by an accomplished rival in the same spirit. The stage to Caroline Chapman was an entire world; she played with all its resources. There remains no record that Lola took the outcome as anything but the fortunes of that warfare in which she seemed perennially engaged.

Seeking an emphatic exit perhaps, early one morning at the Mission Lola Montez had married Patrick Hull, tall, ruddy, likeable enough in a rough fashion, a politician— married him, as she said, because he was the best story- teller she had ever known, and went at once to Sacramento for an engagement. The story of her season there is hardly clear. Every one had now begun the game of burlesquing Lola; the newspapers were full of contradictory stories. According to one tale she marched to the office of an editor who had criticized her, and challenged him to a duel with pistols at five paces or the choice of two tablets in a box, one of which was deadly poison. At least her stay in Sacra- mento was stormy; and her appearance at Marysville suf- fered from an unlucky contrast. A modest young lady vocalist, preceding her by a few days, had captivated the town, singing *Lilly Dale, When the Swallows Homeward*

Fly, Young Ladies, Won't You Marry? and *Woodman, Spare that Tree.* The miners had been melted to tears. The unwonted mood of mildness grew. At a near-by camp they offered the songstress an immense nugget of gold, rough like themselves, they humbly said, and hoped that she would accept it. This was perhaps not the best moment for the spider dance or for a worldly rehearsal of revolutionary life in foreign lands.

So Lola Montez arrived in Grass Valley shorn of glory, trailing sufficient clouds of wickedness. She should have been humble, but she was nothing of the kind. Learning that her dances had been publicly disapproved of by one of the ministers of the village, she donned her ballet costume, threw her cape over her shoulders, dashed up the steps of his house and after a thundering knock flung herself into his presence, danced the tarantella, and demanded at the end, of the bemused gentleman, whether he could observe anything wrong in the spectacle. After such dazzling effrontery and after her spectacular defeat in San Francisco, by any usual human rule of thumb the whole town should have turned against her. But the miners named the highest peak in the range about Grass Valley in her honor—Mount Lola. Within a brief space she had created something of a *salon* in her small cottage, drawing there the liveliest and most interesting of the young men of all nationalities in the village, two of them said to be nephews of Victor Hugo. Music floated out through the windows, of guitars, accordions, violins, with laughter and the sound of animated talk.

"Sometimes the genial spirits would protract their meeting until daybreak," said an elderly woman who placidly set down a description of the hilarity at the cottage more than sixty years afterward with a faint irony for the listener who expected a different tone. "Every new song, every neat story that was read or heard, every bit of eloquence or scrap of humor that any of the young men came across, was preserved for the *salon*. . . . There was champagne, brandy, and wine to drink: all the new fancy drinks were tried there as fast as any one in the company heard of one. Cake, fruit, and occasionally a pudding or a Spanish dish comprised the edibles, and every one smoked." Indeed Lola strolled through the streets smoking, and danced the spider dance in her own house.

By all the rules, at least the women of the village should have outlawed Lola Montez. There was indeed a pause, a struggle; then into the brief chaos stepped a few resolute spirits; and as result Lola continued to do as she chose with only casual criticism, because she was beautiful and unexpected, and because tolerance was abroad in California as an almost explosive element.

Among this group was Mary Ann Crabtree. Perhaps something lawless or romantic was enclosed beneath her own decorous exterior; or her new absorption in theatricals may have drawn her to a figure so recently magnified on

the San Francisco stage. She threw her influence in favor
of the strange Lola, and vigorously praised and defended
her to the end of her days. And Lola Montez responded
with a generous friendship for Mrs. Crabtree and for
other women in the village. Either because it amused her
to do so, or because she liked this rough and rustic haven,
or because something sunny and warm played over the
surface of her feeling, she dissolved antagonism. Like the
other women she worked in her garden and wore calico,
joined her neighbors in needlework, and may be pictured
bending over a sampler. Her cottage was on the road which
led to the school; she invited the children to stop, played
with them, scattered favors, gave extravagant parties for
them at Christmas. With a miner's wife she drove in a
ramshackle old buckboard across the mountains to Dutch
Flat, living on game which they shot or food that they
carried with them. Occasionally on such trips she danced
at camps along the way, and overpassed the stiff pro-
prieties which existed even in the wildest places. According to a local ballad Murietta rebuked her—

> "Joaquin through the mountains was advancing
> When he saw Lola Montez dancing,
> When she danced the spider dance
> He was bound to run her off—"

But gallant or rough robber—according to one's choice—
Murietta was hardly a moralist; and a dozen grisly heads

were now being exhibited in the southern mines as his. Murietta and Lola can hardly have met, and the chances are that if they had, Lola would have had something amusing to say to that elusive character, and that the two would have proved not uncongenial companions for an hour.

With such interludes, Lola maintained a picturesque idyll and played with children. It was small Lotta Crabtree with her red hair, merry black eyes, and irrepressible laugh, of the number racing in and out, who claimed her special interest. Lotta was shy at first, but Mrs. Crabtree let her spend days at a time at Lola's cottage, though as a rule she hardly permitted the child out of her sight. This new juxtaposition was full of oddity. Severely conventional Mrs. Crabtree always was; and all her life Lotta was to preserve an almost incredible innocence. It may be doubted whether she ever knew more than the faint outlines of Lola's career. Yet undoubtedly Lotta grew livelier with her strange new exciting companion. Lola taught her to dance; and though that imperious spirit would never have admitted it, Lotta had a far truer sense of rhythm than Lola herself ever had. Lotta's tiny feet learned the intricacies of a few ballet steps. Liking innovation, Lola had picked up fandangos and highland flings; these too she taught Lotta in sudden gusts of pleasure. From Lola the child learned to sing small ballads; with her she learned to ride horseback. Through the streets of the village, over a lovely hill of color into deep forests, Lola dashed with Lotta on the saddle in front or on a pony at her side. In a blacksmith's shop at Rough and Ready, Lola stood the child on an anvil, clapped her hands, had her dance before a little crowd, and declared that she must go to Paris.

Lotta lost her shyness, and flew in and out among a crowd of strolling players who were steadily drawn to Lola's cottage, and who stayed for an hour or two if they displayed wit or character: if they were dull they quickly departed. An entertainer came through who rang his own bell as he entered each town, beat his own drum, and could impersonate thirty-two different characters, including Webster, Clay, Edwin Forrest, a whole assortment of gold-diggers, Yankee, Dutch, Scotch, Irish, French, with a few representatives from Pike County, Missouri, and a scattering of love-sick damsels. Steve Massett came, the abounding Jeems Pipes of Pipesville, with the last theatrical news from San Francisco, with his own bundle of songs, and a new sheaf of impersonations. Not only Lotta but her mother learned fragments of songs, bits of burlesque, touches of impersonation. Occasionally joining the crowd, Mrs. Crabtree again found herself on the fringe of theatrical life, listening eagerly to theatrical news, fighting its attraction, for at bottom she still distrusted these vagrants.

Early in 1854 theatrical news from San Francisco was

brisk enough. Fortunes in the theaters there, for all their sparkling gayety, had an element of violence. The troupe at the San Francisco, which had seemed impregnable, was scattered. Dr. Robinson had been thrust well into the background. The Chapmans had retreated to Stockton; the American Theatre was closed for lack of business. The theatrical world in San Francisco had been radically and suddenly altered by the appearance of Catherine Sinclair as actress-manager at the new Metropolitan Theatre, which had opened on Christmas Eve, 1853.

From her first appearance Mrs. Sinclair had been enthusiastically received. Her "striking presence," "her fine figure," "her correct study," were mentioned. She was indeed a witty and a charming woman, with a look of firm and gay intention; if she was calculating there was nothing harsh or abrupt in her movements. In her first curtain speech she had made a graceful reference to the hope with which she had turned to the fair land of promise in the West, and added a light allusion to the circumstances which had forced her to labor for subsistence. These circumstances were well known. Like many others she had come wearing her history like an interesting garment.

In the long drawn-out divorce case Mrs. Sinclair had shown a cool head, and had slipped outside Forrest's grasp at every turn. Because of one of his title rôles, he was often likened to a gladiator; he was also described as a roaring bull; and it was Forrest, maddened by jealousy, who had cast a comparatively trivial affair into the public arena. In the struggle which followed Mrs. Sinclair had become the slender adroit *vaquero*, pricking Forrest with fiery goads, and at length triumphing over brute strength. There was tragedy in the encounter, for Forrest never recovered; within that burly exterior was much native fineness and grace, imaged in the delicacy of his dramatic interpretation when he chose to reveal this, and in acts of great generosity and insight. But he was tyrannical; and his fury had increased when after the close of the divorce suit Mrs. Sinclair made a gesture which had the quality of her native wit. Though she came of a theatrical family she had not hitherto appeared on the stage; now she came out in New York in *The School for Scandal*. Here was daring, both in the allusiveness of the chosen play and in the immediacy of her appearance after the long and stormy passage with Forrest. She was a woman, indeed a lady; and persons of her sex had as yet a slight tradition for making such personal—and witty—declarations in public. Indeed her appearance precipitated a brief riot in the theater. But she made a charming Lady Teazle, and undaunted, appeared as Pauline, Margaret Elmore, Lady Macbeth, and Beatrice, while Forrest still fought the judgment awarded her, as he was to fight it for eighteen years.

On the Pacific Coast Mrs. Sinclair displayed the same

*From a painting in the collection of J. Harvey McCarthy,
in the Carthay Circle Theatre, Los Angeles*

LOLA MONTEZ

From a print in the collection of the Society of California Pioneers

SONORA. 1853

lightly suggested initiative. Like Lola Montez she lacked support: but she had quietly set herself to obtain it, playing in first one theater, then another, and traveling to Sacramento, where she gained a further audience. Within a few months she had drawn together a company of her own which included young Edwin Booth, and had secured the managership of the new Metropolitan Theatre. It was rumored that this was built for her use; certainly she might have dictated its splendor.

The Metropolitan—on Montgomery Street—was even more elegantly upholstered in red velvet than any of its predecessors, more opulently decorated in gold, with a velvet drop curtain, tiers of boxes in a horseshoe, and the new extravagance of lighting by coal gas. Here, as if to underscore her first delicate point, Mrs. Sinclair opened in *The School for Scandal*. With an abundance of capital she showered productions and soon bedazzled her public with stars, introducing Matilda Heron who drew to her side the most gilded of the *jeunesse dorée* of the city. Mrs. Sinclair presented the beautiful young Laura Keene, who had made her *début* in London, and had been well received in New York. As her competitors fled from the field, Mrs. Sinclair continued her easy prodigality, producing opera in English, with Mme. Anna Thillon singing the leads in *The Enchantress, The Daughter of the Regiment, The Bohemian Girl,* and *Crown Diamonds.* She brought out the Rousset troupe in ballet, and later the

highly favored Montplaisirs, who had been welcomed in
Paris, New York, Havana, and New Orleans. Bochsa,
one of the great harpists of the century, became her musical director.

Everything was novel, everything brilliant and worldly,
the ballet, these bright phases of the opera, the group of
spirited young actresses, and most of all the spectacle of a
woman on the scene who could contrive and handle all
this profusion. Mrs. Sinclair had seized the honors which
belong to first enterprise. As a manager Laura Keene was
to surpass her in a wider field over a longer period of
years; and Charlotte Cushman had made a brief trial of
management: but to Mrs. Sinclair, single-handed, in a new
region, surrounded by immense handicaps, must go the
palm for the first complete achievement in this country
by a woman as theatrical manager. Finished and intriguing, as a character in the procession of notable characters
she had superseded most of those who had gone before.
As an actress she was less gifted than Caroline Chapman,
with far smaller range, but she had given herself a glam-
orous setting which a gypsy trouper like Caroline Chapman, buffeting all kinds of situations out of sheer amusement, could never acquire. And Lola Montez was doubly
obscured.

To Mary Ann Crabtree, watching and judging, this
spectacle might have been disheartening: but with the rise
of Mrs. Sinclair one conclusion must have been borne in

upon her. The prizes were going to women. In this new world composed preponderantly of men, women were rising to a singular eminence. For months all the drift of interest on the stage had been toward women, Caroline Chapman, Lola Montez, Matilda Heron, Laura Keene, Catherine Sinclair, besides the singers, Biscaccianti, Kate Hayes, and now Anna Bishop. With every lineament of character stressed, indeed indulging to the full any personal caprice, with an air of unusual confidence they had all taken great rewards. It was warfare: higher and higher ran the contention between individuals and companies, between elements in the public. But if the stage in California was still a gusty affair, full of dangerous, sudden changes, it offered an unparalleled opportunity for feminine initiative.

At the moment, early in 1854, another drift in theatricals became clear. There was a high vogue for child actresses. The Bateman children were playing in San Francisco at the Metropolitan, playing everything from *Hamlet* to a California piece written for them by their mother, called *Mother's Trust*. One of the San Francisco newspaper critics had written an irate column on this play, and the father of the Batemans had shot but failed to kill the critic in the Square. The Batemans were still flourishing; and other children, less fortunately introduced, were making their way through Sacramento and in the mines—little Sue Robinson and a bevy of others, scatter-

ing in twos and threes, singing and dancing, as Fairy
Minstrels, Fairy Stars. Some of them had passed through
Grass Valley. All of them were winning great rewards, a
rain of coins and nuggets, as enthusiastic audiences
crowded to see them in every camp. Children were still
unusual figures all through the mountains. At Campton-
ville, no great distance from Grass Valley, miners had
come from miles around on Sunday to see a little girl—
not an actress—who had recently arrived there. Children
who could sing or dance were a delightful novelty.

In a brief pattern Mrs. Crabtree's future lay mapped
before her. Surely she could seize some of the possibilities
of management, with Lotta, who was already trained as
were few of these small troupers. Perhaps Mrs. Crabtree
might not have pressed the matter at once, for in spite
of her alertness she made decisions slowly. Soon she found
that she had no choice. She was halted because she expected the birth of another child. The spring wore away.
In the summer of 1854 a boy was born whom she named
John Ashworth. Then once more Crabtree, who had been
prospecting, painted an irresistible picture. He had been
over the mountains, where new and extraordinarily rich
claims were being opened. Caught perhaps once more by
the hope of a golden windfall, Mrs. Crabtree decided to
make the new venture.

The journey was hard, from Marysville to Bidwell's
Bar by stage, then by pack-mule through forests, up nar-

row trails above a branch of the Feather River to Little
Grass Valley, and on to the busy camp of Rabbit Creek, set
on a tiny plateau beneath a looming peak above. It was a
violent small camp, hemmed in by snows in winter, now
loosed to headlong energies with the coming of spring
and the discovery of pocket after pocket of rich gold.
Murder was as frequent here as in most remote camps.
"Money was the object of the friends who perpetrated
the affair," said a brief newspaper note on a sudden death.
The bystanders were so "exasperated," ran an account of
another episode, "that they lynched the man."

The temper of the new camp had grown fierce in a
summer of unusually intense drouth, when water was
lacking to wash gold. Crabtree got nothing. The weather
was too dry; rougher characters reached the ground before him; he worked too little, spent too many hours at
the camp bars, or roamed off no one knew where. Crabtree was a vigorous man, who chose what he wanted and
kept to his choice. If there had ever been a doubt before
what this was it was clear enough henceforward. Crabtree wanted unobstructed leisure. When winter closed
down again his wife was obliged to turn to the sole means
of living which lay ready before her. Once more she managed a boarding-house, under far greater difficulties than
before, ruder in surroundings, with all roads cut off.

In the spring Lola Montez rode over the mountains,
taking the high abrupt trail to Downieville through thick

forests, dipping into cleft valleys. She had grown restless at last, and meant to go to Australia. Every one wondered why she had remained so long in seclusion at Grass Valley. Rumors were abroad of a fantastic political scheme by which she was to become Empress of California in a seceded empire. At least a faint token came down the years of such a wild enterprise. Morose and violent, she had clashed with the editor of a Nevada City newspaper who, adding a slurred allusion to herself, had criticized some unfortunate strolling players whom she had befriended. Whether or not she horsewhipped him remains a question, but at least a furor arose that reverberated along the Coast.

Lola Montez had a purpose beyond that of saying farewell in coming to Rabbit Creek. Realizing the straitened circumstances of the Crabtrees, she hoped to take Lotta with her to Australia. Mrs. Crabtree's refusal was sharp. Lola returned alone to Grass Valley, and was soon off to Australia with her maid Periwinkle and a young actor named Folland, followed by a measured and generous encomium in the Grass Valley *Telegraph*, which acknowledged her vagaries and praised her character. She was to return to California within a year.

To such a proposal as Lola had just made Mrs. Crabtree would always have given a passionate reply. Now she had every reason for a refusal. Events had moved. In the midst of the roaring life at Rabbit Creek was a young

Italian who went under the name of Mart Taylor, and was something of a musician, a dancer, a versifier, and a cobbler. Lotta, who grew fond of him, said long afterwards that he had come to California "with all kinds of air castles packed up in his carpet-bag. They toppled over as soon as he set them up, and he fell back upon music for a living." Taylor ran a saloon, where music was abundant, and a little log theater, where he sometimes joined with traveling players, and a dancing school for the few small children of the camp. He was accomplished in jigs and reels, and added to Lotta's repertoire of steps. The child's dancing had begun to attract attention in the camp when Dr. Robinson appeared there with small Sue Robinson in his train. He had at once demanded to see Lotta. With a table for a stage, and Sue grinding a hand-organ for music, Lotta danced a *cracovienne* which she had learned from Lola Montez with lively dash and spirit.

The tiny red-haired girl with her bright eyes and quick light feet, her command of intricate steps and a complicated rhythm, could hardly have failed to impress an experienced theatrical manager. Lotta was now nearly eight years old, but she looked hardly six; to audiences eager to see children her diminutive size would prove an irresistible attraction. The chances were strong that Dr. Robinson would have engaged Lotta then or later, when a difficulty arose with Mart Taylor. Robinson considered that Taylor asked too much for the use of his theater for an evening's performance, and decided to play in a dance hall across the road. By way of retaliation Taylor put on an entertainment of his own the same night with Lotta as a child star in opposition to Sue.

Mrs. Crabtree was obliged to make a hard decision. She had given up the boarding-house; she was ready to make a change. She had had plenty of opportunity to reflect on the power of the witty and engaging Dr. Robinson in San Francisco and elsewhere. Nor is it likely that he showed the effects of the recent rapid clashes in San Francisco among the theaters. Dr. Robinson never lost his high spirits and resilience. No doubt Lotta's rise to recognition would have been far easier and swifter if she had had him as a guide. But Mrs. Crabtree made a definite turning and took the more difficult road, obeying a passionate instinct to keep her child's career in her own hands.

With flying fingers she made Lotta a tiny long-tailed green coat, knee breeches, a tall green hat. Taylor cobbled her a pair of brogans. She came on the stage with a miniature shillelagh, pleased with her new costume; and since she knew every one in the audience she was not shy. Casting aside the shillelagh, the absurd midget danced an Irish jig and a reel. She always had a way of laughing when she danced, hard enough to achieve by design when every breath counts, but natural for her. She seemed tireless, a tiny bubbling fountain of fun and quick life. On the rough stage with candles for footlights in the midst of smoke and shadows she danced again and again; every other number was forgotten, even Taylor's dancing and singing. Then she appeared in a white dress with a round neck and puffed sleeves, and sang a plaintive, innocent ballad, looking like a pretty little red-haired doll.

The smoke-laden room was shaken with excitement. Money rained upon the stage: quarters, half dollars, huge Mexican dollars, a fifty-dollar gold slug, and a scattering of nuggets. The camp at Rabbit Creek had rallied round Taylor in the contest with Dr. Robinson, or had strolled into the theater as the applause thundered. The resourceful little doctor was defeated and retired, leaving Mary Ann Crabtree to consider her child's success. She now possessed more money than she had had at any time in California. The next step seemed inevitable. She accepted Taylor's quick sketch of the luck which must come to a small traveling troupe, and while Crabtree was in the mountains learned to play that quaint instrument, the triangle. Taylor insisted that they must have plenty of music. He found a violinist, and he himself could play the guitar. He taught Lotta a further string of pretty ballads and a few appealing songs like *How Can I Leave Thee?* His own songs were parodies in the vein which Dr. Robinson had made popular, by which the miners were betrayed into laughing at themselves. Taylor had a genuine gift for rhymed improvisation, and with a line or a question from his audience could throw almost any event into song—

> "Old P. T. Barnum had the rocks
>   Few days, few days,
> But lost them all on wooden clocks—
> I'm going home.

> "He bragged about his luck too soon
>   A few days, a few days,
> For now he hasn't a picayune—
> I'm going home."

A tall man, he looked the stroller, almost the troubadour, with hair as long and as jetty as the plumage of a Stockton blackbird, piercing black eyes, and an Oriental grace of figure and cast of countenance.

On a morning of late spring the new company started out in a wagon during one of Crabtree's absences. Lotta was at her mother's side, Ashworth in her arms. Left behind in the cabin were some loaves of fresh bread, a pot of beans, and a note. There was more than one effect of personal signature in these objects. The note was brief, and perhaps final. The beans and the bread were left to provide for Crabtree, but they had none the less a look of uncommon firmness. The signature which Mrs. Crabtree left behind was hardly less positive than that which she carried in her look and presence. She was still a pretty woman, but the impervious air which she had always been able to assume had grown more definite during her two years in California. In joining Taylor and the violinist she had made a difficult choice. Even in the midst of the free standards of the Coast women still drew an inevitable criticism. Mrs. Crabtree ignored the possibility. One fancies her sitting bolt upright in the wagon with her children as they started out, with a look of neat inscrutability, bent only upon the new, precarious business of entertainment.

The camp at Rabbit Creek lay near the crossing of six trails, leading to the City of Seventy-Six, Port Wine, Rich Bar, Gibsonville, Quincy, Bidwell's Bar. The company went first in the direction of Quincy, changing from the wagon to mules as they struck the high rugged trails. Accoutered with red, blue, and yellow tassels and trappings, the mules suggested a holiday journey. But for Mrs. Crabtree at least there was terror in this change, as the beasts picked their way on tiny feet along dizzy precipices, following the leader's tinkling bell. Since mules were seldom skittish with women or even with small girls if they were quiet, Lotta was strapped to the back of one of them. Mrs. Crabtree, carrying her small boy in her arms or holding him before her on the saddle, was also fastened in place to give her greater freedom with her child. By long halters each mule was tied to the one ahead. As the little procession skirted high cliffs along steep and narrow winding trails each rider often turned out of sight of the others. They were frequently obliged to pass long pack trains on pebbly oblique paths. Unfriendly Indians were said to lurk in the denser, more northerly forests. If attacks from these were known to be few, there was always danger from highwaymen who roamed through the mountains. The company was obliged to ride in silence.

Lotta, already accustomed to horses, became almost at once a fearless small rider, and even learned to sleep in the saddle at night when the company was in haste to reach a new camp in time to make preparations for a coming performance. The high mountain air was clear and exhilarating. In the late spring and early summer there was beauty both delicate and robust in these places, with white lilies and a drift of syringa, irises of many colors, and a fragrant flower like breaking clusters of seed-pearl, the Spanish *libla*. High above towered the peaks of the Sierras, snow-powdered. Down in some deep valley might be seen tiny men bent and toiling over the match-like splinter of flumes beside the still rush of rivers, crimson at their borders from the wash of gold.

As they neared a new camp Taylor whistled and sang, and the company would rest for an hour so as to make their entry with the look of fatigue smoothed away, with an air of pleasure and high spirits. Then Taylor went ahead, beating the drum. His tall wild figure and easy grace would have gained them an instant hearing in any mining village even if its inhabitants had not seen Lotta following, perched on the back of her mule. Children had not yet found their way into the high mountain camps; and few players of any kind came so far into the interior. By the presence of Lotta an almost riotous success was assured in every cloth and paper town they entered.

They played in bar-rooms; and since many a bar was the village store, the troupe put on their entertainment in the midst of smoked ham and canned meats, red and blue flannel shirts strung across a line, and mining implements stacked by a counter. Crimson calico was everywhere, arranged in broad flutings around mirrors that had been triumphantly brought by pack-train up the mountains. Red calico was strung as curtains at the windows and draped over bunks built in the side-walls. A small stage would be contrived at the end of a low room by boards set on saw-horses, or even by tying two billiard tables together, with woolen blankets hung in front for curtains. A few candles stuck in bottles guttered in front. Taylor, with his tall figure, was frequently obliged to adapt his acts to a sitting position.

Lotta was shy in these strange places, confronting an audience—mostly men—whom she had never seen. As she learned that a routine of dancing and singing lay before her the child seldom wished to appear. For an hour before the entertainment her mother, both resolute and lively, with her other child to tend, would coax, tell her funny stories, try to make a game of the coming performance. At the right moment, given a little push, Lotta would go out or be lifted to the stage, fall in with the music and dance her jigs and reels with her irresistible look of merriment. As soon as she was well in the midst of her act there was no doubt of her pleasure. A sturdy little girl, she would rollic over a tiny stage, whisk the coattails of the ridiculous little green suit, and even become, as her mother thought, rather rowdy, sticking her hands in her pockets. At last Mrs. Crabtree sewed them up. Trying to find them in the midst of a jig, Lotta was hindered, stopped, burst into tears, and ran crying off the stage, sobbed until the sewing was ripped out, and then came back with flushed cheeks and a small red nose, to finish her number. At the end of each performance, with hair smoothed, fresh and clean, she would appear in white cambric to sing her ballad. Nuggets would be showered upon her in profusion, often falling so fast that the child was frightened and Mrs. Crabtree was obliged to gather them up afterward in a basket, sweeping and scraping every fragment or little pile of gold dust.

The company moved continually, from tiny camp to camp, scouring every known cluster of cabins in this rich region. By a long criss-cross through the mountains they at length dipped toward Rich Bar, set in a narrow valley hardly a thousand yards long at the base of lofty hills which were almost perpendicular, a wild little camp where clashes between the Spaniards and the Americans of the region, stabbing affrays, thefts, lynchings, riots, whippings, had been frequent for several years. Few women were there, though perhaps the Indiana Girl remained, whose hugely resonant voice had been heard rolling through two closed doors and down a long entry in a hotel, and who often packed fifty pounds of flour on her back over the mountains.

Here was a strangely colored hotel, designed originally for two women of pleasure, a rambling place whose rooms were lined with purple calico or a delicate and aerial blue, with floors covered by fine matting—floors that ran unevenly from room to room, so that the whole structure seemed a flimsy crazy dream. Even the doors were colored, of blue drilling on frames with leather hinges. If this place had gone up in the almost inevitable fire before the Taylor troupe arrived, another hardly less bizarre would have housed them. Bars had multiplied: the Oriental, the Golden Gate, the Don Juan. Claret had become as common as water. The place had changed little enough since Dame Shirley lived there, a delicate perceptive woman who had been a schoolmate of Emily Dickinson. Equably enough she had described a wild supper when a company of men had kept up an orgy of dancing for three nights. In almost Falstaffian terms she had written of another festival begun by a procession in which the

Chileans reeled with better grace, she said, the Americans more naturally.

In this region Mrs. Crabtree and her children were obliged to lie on the floor of their room one night while bullets tore through the canvas walls during a brawl which moved in and out of the hotel. Long afterward she wove her own narratives of such affairs with calm detail. In the midst of her new enterprise, when everything depended on her coolness and good spirits—for Lotta must remain lively and happy—with hard travel before her, and many a minor matter of decorum to observe if she was to keep a sufficient dignity, she mechanically noted the look and color of innumerable small experiences and stored them away.

Some of her listeners in later years thought that her stories verged upon literature. She had a fashion of stripping them down to unvarnished essentials, and delivered them in a rich throaty voice which always seemed charged with incompleted emotion. But Mrs. Crabtree was never concerned with literature or with any art. In these years and afterward she was a woman with heavy responsibilities which she could not forget. Mingled with all these dangerous sharp experiences was a sense of uneasiness which came from something more than any immediate danger. Had she made the right choice in taking this long uncharted tour? For herself? For Lotta? What else could she have done? What lay ahead? Such questions dinned themselves into her mind as she traveled, as she prepared the child for her acts, and she herself struck the bent steel of the triangle.

As the troupe went on to Bidwell's Bar, still on mule-back, they followed a precipice miles long, looking down among the blue-green pines to a broken chain of tiny lakes that wavered and grew hard and dazzling in the heat. At Bidwell's Bar heat smote them. The town boasted a thea-ter, but Taylor and his companions could hardly have hoped to play there; traveling companies of considerable pretensions frequently came to Bidwell's Bar. Taylor's troupe was obliged to play in the usual hotel or bar-room, and to travel by night to the surrounding camps. The region was immensely rich; beneath white rapids the bar, dense with gold, was yielding returns that seemed inexhaustible. The town had been nearly undermined by gold-diggers. For a small troupe there were advantages in playing in this heat-ridden place and in accepting the smaller houses of entertainment. These cost little or noth-ing; the returns were lavish. To Mrs. Crabtree's insistent questions came a steadily growing answer in the nuggets and money and gold dust which she now carried.

At Oroville too they found a theater, with private boxes, a gallery, and a considerable equipment of scenery: but they could hardly have commanded it, and must have played as before in the smaller places. Here perhaps they learned that the more traveled parts of the mountains had been full of theatrical companies. The Roussets had offered their exquisite ballets and pantomimes on little stages from Sonora to Grass Valley all through the summer of 1855. The first widespread entry of talented actors into the mining camps had begun. If there seemed luck and comfort for Mrs. Crabtree in the circumstance that she had made the same choice as far better-known players, the consolation after all must have been slight. She had grown increasingly tired. The heat on this lower level remained intense. But the troupe must have ranged about Oroville for several weeks, for it was autumn when they found themselves well northward at Weaverville, traveling at last by stage.

Little steamers ran from Sacramento to Red Bluffs. Stages followed the main routes toward Shasta. Once again Taylor's company was entering a region frequently traversed by theatrical companies. A well-known troupe, undistinguished but capable, which had been in California for many months and was to remain many more, had established a circuit to the north which included Shasta, Weaverville, Eureka, and other mining towns. They were being received by crowded houses.

The small company in which Lotta was the leading figure must have crept into Weaverville as a minor diversion. Yet Lotta, who had now learned to dance with even greater vivacity than before, to romp with greater freedom and sing her ballads with readier smiles or solemn look of tears, now carved for herself a tiny lasting niche in local tradition. But for Mrs. Crabtree these days must have been filled with something bordering upon despair. She had known for many weeks as she traveled that long route from camp to camp over the mountains what she had not known when she left Rabbit Creek, that she was to bear another child.

She was obliged to stop playing. The company broke up. Taylor, a loyal friend, took Ashworth to San Francisco. Asking about responsible people near at hand into whose care she might give Lotta, Mrs. Crabtree learned of James Talbot Ryan of Eureka, a pioneer there, and sent her to his family. For Lotta the trip was a wild one, through heavily wooded country in wet weather with a stranger on horseback: but in the friendly household at Eureka she frolicked and sang—"I've a howl in my heart big enough to roll a cabbage round in"—and went through her acts as in a game for the other children.

Mrs. Crabtree seldom spoke of the brief passage which followed for herself. Whether her child was born in Weaverville or in some neighboring village is not clear. After all hers was not an uncommon lot among women of the stage playing in the mountains. In that scattered community of theater people, so transiently here and there, the larger routine of life went on as in more settled situations. Many women played until they could play no longer, and contrived something like a brief domestic hearth for a few weeks in some strange log hotel or flimsy canvas boarding-house. The difference was that Mrs. Crabtree was alone, and that every touch of tradition which she possessed was at war with the situation in which she found herself. Among strangers the child came at last, another boy, whom she named George. As soon as she could travel she followed the wet and wintry trail to Eureka, remained there for a time with the Ryans, then, in the spring of 1856, taking Lotta and the baby, sailed from the narrow bay in a small schooner for San Francisco.

Far less buoyantly than before she confronted the city, and found it larger, bolder in outline, with more substantial buildings, longer wharves, a more hurried and more formidable life. The town was full of stormy legend. The months just past had seen a succession of tempests, with a climax in the shooting of Richardson and of James King of William, the gusty rise of the second Vigilance Committee, the preparatory siege of Fort Gunnybags. For a young woman with a prim heart like Mrs. Crabtree, whose burdens had now greatly increased, this dark and seething tumult must have seemed a threat. She had chosen the life of the theater, with misgivings; and theaters now seemed a special arena for violence.

Within the few months past, in the smaller gambling saloons and exchanges which offered dancing numbers and minstrel acts, one clash after another had occurred. It was

in a theater that the personal collision had taken place
which had precipitated the formation of the Vigilance
Committee. During an evening of pantomime and extravaganza at the American a man had turned to stare at
Belle Cora, who with her husband, Charles Cora the
gambler, occupied one of the boxes. There was no more
doubt of the vocation which Belle Cora promoted than
that which her husband openly pursued. But fable surrounded her; she was a dark and pensive beauty who was
said to have come from a good family in New Orleans.
Cora was slight and supple, with dark eyes that had a
melancholy look; from his habitual black and his flowing
collar he might have been taken for a young poet who
had seldom considered anything more worldly than a
rhyme. At the theater the stranger had turned again and
stared at Belle Cora. As a rule, women of her station
occupied curtained stalls at the rear of the house. Unfortunately this intrusive glance seemed to be directed
toward the wife of United States Marshal Richardson.

Later, in a brief encounter between Richardson and
Cora on the streets, Cora had shot Richardson dead. The
mistrial of Cora had led to other violence, out of which
the Vigilance Committee had arisen. Cora and Casey had
been hanged: but violence was still abroad, with an
extraordinary medley of romantic standards. Belle Cora
was already beginning to assume the place which she was
to occupy in the popular mind for many years, as a myste-

rious. and tragic figure. Women of the underworld had a part in two other episodes that had brought the city close to a state of war. San Francisco was caught in an emotional and civic turmoil.

Nor had the life of the players there during the few months just past been more peaceful than the external life which had milled and fought through its thoroughfares. Theatrical warfare had been more graceful, but none the less drastic. No position could have seemed more stable than that of Mrs. Sinclair after the brilliance of her opening months at the Metropolitan. But even during the panic of 1855 she had maintained a reckless pace of production which looked like sheer willfulness. After her first successes with opera she had seemed satisfied with nothing but operatic ventures; she had attempted to produce opera in San Francisco over a period of nearly eighteen months, when continuance through less than half that period would have represented a signal success in any city in the country. She was gallant, she was resourceful: public favor had remained with her for a time as a kind of personal tribute. But her public at last showed with emphasis that what it wanted was not opera but plays.

"The fiat of the San Francisco public has gone forth against opera," declared one writer. The obdurate Mrs. Sinclair had been conquered at last only by a lack of money and a surplusage of temperament on the part of a company of Italian singers, the Barili-Thornes. A public quarrel occurred over a trunkful of costumes which were said to belong to Mrs. Sinclair, and a matter of carriage-hire for one of the singers. The quarrel became *opéra bouffe*, and was continued by means of lively cards in the newspapers and even on the stage of the Metropolitan before an almost empty house. Mrs. Sinclair was at last constrained to retire. Perhaps she had given form to some fantasy of her own in her career as manager, yet there must have been bitterness in her defeat, for her stubborn ambition had permitted the rise of Laura Keene.

San Francisco was demanding plays, and Laura Keene lavishly produced them. High-tempered, warm-hearted, with what one of her admirers called a grim humor about herself, quite alone, she had plunged into management after her return from Australia. She had promptly gathered a capable company—which changed rapidly enough under her high-mettled leadership—and like Mrs. Sinclair had gained the setting of a new theater, the finely constructed new American. Like her predecessor, she had indulged her own taste, which tended to be literary and delicate.

The strange circumstance was that in the darkening mood of the city, with all the passionate and brutal exigencies which were leading to the formation of the Vigilance Committee of 1856, Laura Keene's offerings had had an immense popularity. Her long season at the American had been rich in classical plays. She had given

the most ample and varied productions of Shakespeare
the city had yet seen, half a dozen performances of
Hamlet, as many of *Macbeth,* and *Richard III.* She produced *Othello, Much Ado,* even *Coriolanus.* Perhaps it
was in the poetic comedies of Shakespeare that she found
the fullest scope for her talents, most of all in *Midsummer Night's Dream.* If she gave the play more than a
dash of extravagance, her control of a graceful profusion
seemed to bring it near perfection, elaborate indeed with
all the gilded embellishment of the time, yet lightly magical, with an exemplary ease of movement.

All Laura Keene's fine productions had been repeated
many times, and were interspersed with the extravaganzas,
each as splendidly mounted as her more ambitious plays.
She had brought out *The Naiad Queen* in a new and
gorgeous version, *The Black Cook, The Flying Horse,*
and the gay and startling *Deep, Deep Sea, or the American Sea Serpent,* which required a regiment of players for
the cast, new mountings throughout for the many scenes,
and was based on the story of Perseus and Andromeda,
with a native twist, a broad touch of local fun, and a few
transformations into sheer circus.

Laura Keene had left for the Atlantic States at the peak
of her triumph, in the late autumn, but Mrs. Crabtree had
reached San Francisco in time to feel its impact. Occasionally, with some weariness, she must have concluded
that she was destined to weave in and out among notable

careers. She seemed to keep the knack of appearing when
theatrical effects were at their height, or when the larger
figures were marching by. The discouraging circumstance
was that they all seemed to be so quickly gone. Not one
of the figures of the stage whom she had watched after
her arrival two years before had remained entrenched in
the city except Tom Maguire and the strong-minded Mrs.
Judah, who was always in demand. Maguire, silent and
secure, straight as a pike-handle, was now drifting about,
morosely pleased with the rise of a new company of
minstrels at the San Francisco.

Mrs. Crabtree might easily have slipped into a period
of respite at this time. She still had a considerable accumulation of money from the summer's travel. Her baby was
small. But either a sense of future necessity, or the new
possession of gold, or even something relentlessly attrac-
tive in the life of the trouper, drew her forth. She lin-
gered hardly at all in San Francisco. For a woman of less
initiative the obvious thing would have been to turn again
to the kind of entertainment which had already brought
considerable rewards. Instead, she took a small leaf out
of Laura Keene's book. Plays were in demand; she determined upon legitimate theatricals for Lotta. It was not
for nothing that she had picked up every scrap of theatrical news, or that she had watched and listened intently at
the theaters in San Francisco two years before. With her
own gift of mimicry and a keen eye for dramatic possi-

bilities, she had perhaps observed these in Lotta, as the child had grown more confident on the small impromptu stages of the mining camps. How she made an entry for Lotta into the obscure theatrical company which they presently joined is not plain. Perhaps it was by sheer persistent skirmishing, or through players, now forgotten, whose paths had crossed hers in the more frequented mountain camps. Lotta's parts were leagues removed from the brilliant repertoire of which they had lately heard so much. The plays were worn farces. But audiences had enjoyed watching the little red-haired girl dance; they might be amused by the novelty of seeing her romp through grown-up rôles. The new company was to travel. Mrs. Crabtree left Ashworth in the care of friends, and with Lotta and the tiny George started out once more in summer for a short tour in the Valley of the Moon.

IV

THE MERRY MINERS

THE NEW COMPANY SET OUT FROM SAN FRANCISCO BY schooner, sailing across the bay, finding the entrance to the Petaluma Creek, half hidden from view among low flats and broken slopes. Up the narrow tortuous channel ships of shallow draft could sail only at high tide. They wound their way among pale gold conical hills, passed other light craft within speaking distance, and sat on deck —for these small schooners had no cabins—their musical instruments at their sides, their tiny store of costumes in champagne baskets. Even Mrs. Crabtree made the concession of using this dubious gay mode, which most traveling actors followed. With her look of domesticity, her baby in her arms and Lotta within call, she listened imperturbably to the stage gossip of the day.

Every one was hearing of the sad fortunes of young Edwin Booth. After his first real success in California, playing *The Marble Heart* in Sacramento the winter before, Booth had set out again for the mountains, traveling with mediocre players, riding with a wagon show, posting his own bills, beating his own drum. Ill luck had pursued them all. Two members of the company had taken with them a gorgeous wardrobe, relics of better days, with costumes of satin and velvet, feathers, bits of ermine, and other paraphernalia; but fire swept Nevada City when they played there; all their possessions were lost. Strangely enough, wherever the company went, fires broke out. Fairy Stars—children like Lotta—were now playing all through the mines. Booth was dubbed the Fiery Star. The news traveled; the company became unwelcome in mountain camps. At Downieville the rumble of threats was heard; and ropes still dangled from the limb of a tree, tokens of a recent summary execution. Booth decided to quit the place; but the manager of his company was already in debt in Downieville, and Booth's horse was seized for payment as he was leaving. He was said to be on his way to Sacramento on foot.

What lay before the little company of which Lotta and her mother were a part was doubtful, but at least in Petaluma they were not obliged to improvise a stage. The tiny, low-lying village had a small theater upstairs in a wooden building, equipped with boxes and even a parquette. Here Lotta made her first dramatic appearance, at the age of nine, as Gertrude in *A Loan of a Lover*, a simple comedy with stiff action and a forced ending which was still a favorite in New York after twenty years of hard service. Sturdy and full of laughter, Lotta vigorously pursued the stupid Spuyk, reaching for a lover as any child might reach for a sugar-plum. Alone on the stage she broke into jigs or reels as if she could not help it. She followed with an equally absurd part in *The Dumb Belle*.

Her coach was her mother, who knew nothing about the theater except what she had learned from quick and curious observation during her two brief sojourns in San Francisco, or from traveling players whom she had chanced to see in Grass Valley, or during the long hard jaunt of the summer before. But she understood sharply studied effects. Somehow she knew what would draw laughter; and she knew how to arouse the sprite of laughter in her little girl. In one play Lotta had only to place a bottle on a table. Mrs. Crabtree taught her to peer from the wings, to withdraw, set one foot forward, to walk across the stage bearing the bottle with exaggerated dignity, and then to laugh—with a look at the audience—as she set it down. It was the inconsequent quick laugh—so unexpectedly hearty for her size—and the companionable glance that drew a response.

After the first performance an older actress demanded the part; but Mrs. Crabtree had stipulated that Lotta was to keep it, and she not only could make a bargain, she could enforce one. Lotta continued to walk on with the bottle, added a jig step as she set it down, and turned a handspring as she reached the wings again. By the time Mrs. Crabtree had completed her enhancement of the tiny rôle, it stood out almost as a separate act. She may have disrupted the play, but most members of the striving small company were seeking an equal notice. Every eye was riveted on the child from the moment she poked her small red head from the wings until the last whisk of her skirts was seen. Audiences watched for her, shouted and flung money to her on the stage. Once when she toiled to pick up the pieces one of her stockings ripped; she still had the fat little legs of childhood; the crowd laughed. Lotta's response was quick and personal. She stamped her foot at them and ran off crying. She could be coaxed to go back. She was always flying out for one small turn or another, appearing briefly for a song or dance even when she was not acting in the main play or the after-piece.

Profits were good as the company traveled about the Valley of the Moon. Mrs. Crabtree perhaps had the heartening conviction that Lotta had made a beginning in the legitimate theater. Even the boards on which she played were substantial, the audience formally placed instead of being crowded in a hit or miss fashion around a makeshift stage of tables and saw-horses. Mrs. Crabtree's expectations for the future had lifted when they returned to San Francisco in the late summer; but they were soon dashed again. Maguire had marched into prominence once more; and Maguire, who had always had an obscure passion for music, had thrown his lot with minstrelsy. That thrum of the banjo and blackface interchange which had

begun in the gambling saloons were now to be heard in
full force at the San Francisco Theatre, and abundantly
elsewhere in the city. The *Ham Fat Man* was being
hummed on every side. One minstrel had been presented
with gold-tipped bones. Nearly every celebrated figure of
early minstrelsy had now arrived in California: Birch,
Bernard, Wells, Backus, Coes, Eph Horn, the Buckleys,
and at least one of the famous Christys. Some of them had
traveled on the show-boat *Banjo* up and down the Mississippi. Many of them had been playing in California for
several years, taking on a gradually increased prominence,
mixing in rapidly shifted, highly competitive companies.

Powerful, noisy figures, they kept to the older plantation type of negro character, with rolling and tumbling.
They were versatile in impersonation, fluent in burlesque.
In a single performance one of the Buckleys could burlesque an orchestra concert on a kitchen bellows, give a
bones solo, play the banjo, imitate with bones the sound
of drums, march, and reveille, and conclude with an imi-
tation of two horses running a race. Operatic burlesque
was a favorite minstrel springboard; nearly every operatic
venture in San Francisco had been turned into blackface
extravaganza with opulent action and by-play. Two huge
minstrel festivals had been held, one company pitted
against another. The mining public, having been richly
diverted by numbers of theatrical productions for half
a dozen years, was astir with an exuberant response to

this expansive entertainment. Its many-sided music, its wide range of moods, plaintive or wild, its lively dancing, and fresh topical dialogue had caught an ample popular fancy.

Mrs. Crabtree, anxiously scanning the theatrical scene, must have found these new and dominant companies terrifying. To the end of her days she never regarded any company with favor, except as a slight and secondary background for Lotta. She saw only Lotta. But this new drift in the theater was unmistakable. The jingle of minstrelsy must have echoed in her mind as she tried to find the child a place or a part where she might have her effective hour or even half-hour. She approached the silent stalking figure of Maguire, as did every one else in the theatrical world unless ranged in bitter opposition. But Maguire, absorbed in his San Francisco Minstrels, was not interested in children. After a few weeks of canvassing Mrs. Crabtree was obliged to take slight and inconsiderable engagements for Lotta in auction rooms along the bay.

Perched on a barrel or a table, her small red head bobbing well above the crowd, Lotta sang and danced, attracted the attention of passers-by, and filled in brief intervals while an auctioneer made ready for his noisy patter or prepared to sell his collection of Chinese shawls, Spanish chests, or mahogany furniture. She kept these engagements and advanced to others, more coveted but dubious,

From the Harvard Theatre Collection

CATHERINE SINCLAIR

From a painting by H. Walton, 1857, in the possession of Mrs. R. M. Gregg

ROUGH AND READY

at the Bella Union, which had been the scene of brief bits
of entertainment from the days of '49, when an unlucky
bones had been shot there.

Into those bright saloons, where men of chequered history gathered, where cards were dealt by gayly dressed
women of uncertain antecedents, Mrs. Crabtree whisked
her child for a brief act, and whisked her away again before the gaudy scene could leave its print. More than ever
she must have had her doubts and questions. There was
indeed the slight barrier of the stage between Lotta and
her audience, but it was part of the child's special gift that
she continually broke this down, taking the onlookers into
her small confidence, sharing her unmistakable fun. It
was Mrs. Crabtree who made the final stockade, and drew
about Lotta that ring of disconcerting fire that was to
surround her for many years, perhaps for the remainder
of her life.

Hers was a strange impulse, that kept the child so
closely to herself, yet so tirelessly before a mixed public.
Grimly resolute, she cultivated humor, because it would
pay, perhaps because of some hidden fund of amusement
within herself which seemed destined to find no other
outlet. She had in fact receded into the position which she
was to occupy for years, that of Lotta's mother, Lotta's
manager, the dragon who made the bargains and guarded
the rewards. If there was irony in this situation, Mrs.
Crabtree had a taste for irony. The humor she gave to

Lotta. She could continually pour warmth and vivacity and a challenging fun into the child, who caught and tossed it back, if not to her mother, then to her audience, with an air of playing some preposterous game. Her small battledore and shuttlecock at the Bella Union was so successful, her dancing so spirited and accomplished that she wove herself into the tradition of the place, where only the liveliest talent was tolerated, where actors of all kinds were put to a severe test if they were to please that skeptical and high-pitched changing public. Into those brilliant rooms Lotta went again and again, danced amid the tinkle of bells, the music of guitars, following minstrel acts, coming on before a bit of tumbling, showered with gold by the invading miners.

In spite of her popularity nothing else was offered. She still took day-by-day dancing engagements along the waterfront. For more ambitious acts, for parts in plays, Mrs. Crabtree searched in vain. They slipped again into obscurity. In the midst of the rising strains of minstrelsy public attention was now occupied once more by the rise and clash of well-known figures of the earlier stage. Lola Montez had returned from Australia; and Caroline Chapman had come forward, her brilliant ancient enemy.

The long season of Lola Montez in Australia had begotten a multitude of legends, fusing into a single effect, that of her violence. Tales of her temper or her horse-whippings had sprung up like nettles. Her spider dance was said to have been forbidden in Melbourne. Still hard and dazzling, on her return she showed an underlying pensiveness beneath her lawless air. Folland, the actor who had accompanied her to Australia, had been drowned on the return voyage; some persons believed that he had committed suicide; many observed that Lola felt herself responsible. She had taken a small iron house, had hung gay cages with many-colored birds about the rooms, and walked through the streets with a magnificent white talking cockatoo perched on her shoulder and a pack of dogs at her heels. Women professed themselves terrified as she appeared in the Square with the great white bird aloft beside her dark head. Both wilder and more gentle, she seemed as aimless in these promenades as in her career: but she soon showed a positive purpose.

She walked straight into the warring camp. The Chapmans, back from the mines, were in control at the American Theatre. Whether through their proposed mischief or through Lola's own vigorous will, she appeared there ten days after she landed, as Mrs. Chillington in *The Morning Call* with William Chapman opposite, and instantly won the allegiance of the critics. Every one remarked the enhanced quality of her acting. But the inevitable sequel occurred, as perhaps Lola had foreseen that it would. On an off night the Chapmans offered the burlesque. This time the tide turned unmistakably against them. Silence or resentment followed. The travesty was

considered "ungallant," "unchivalrous." "There probably
never was, and never will be, an actress in San Francisco
who has made more friends and admirers than Caroline
Chapman," wrote one gentleman, and contended that
Miss Chapman had debased her talents.

On the heels of this episode Lola Montez sold her collection of jewelry at auction for the benefit of Folland's
two children; this included many diamond bracelets, a
dozen or more diamond rings, some rubies, among them
a magnificent pigeon-blood, jeweled crosses, pendants, a
jeweled comb, lockets, necklaces, and a basketful of heavy
pieces made of Australian gold. Perhaps something of a
traced design within her life was apparent even to herself
at this moment. Meeting a mixed fate, she had often
seemed to bestow great misfortune: an ill chance had
befallen Ludwig of Bavaria, Dujarrier, Folland, perhaps
others. Southwick, whom she had known well at Grass
Valley, was now ill and unfriended. Hull was already in
a decline, was soon to be in actual want and was to die
prematurely. Two years later—did she ever know it?—
Shipley committed suicide.

On the eve of the auction, like a rude bit of mocking
laughter, the unregenerate Chapmans produced a new
burlesque, so ample in scope that it occupied the bill for
an entire evening, called *A Trip to Australia, or Lola
Montez on the Fanny Major*. This broad slash at Lola's
intended charity met an unmitigated condemnation. But

the Chapmans were a stubborn pair, still acting within that close bond which had held them as a family since childhood; their daring was as sharp as Lola's though of a more realistic order: plainly they suspected their erstwhile companion of histrionics in her public auction of jewels for charity; and they continued the play in spite of the critics.

But Caroline Chapman no longer possessed the vivacity which could carry her through a full length play, an afterpiece, and several *entr'actes* of dancing or singing in the course of a single evening; nor could she appear in new plays nightly. With the exception of the new burlesque, the bills at the American lacked the novelty which with her brother she had offered with so free a hand in their first months on the Coast. The old plays were repeated. Miss Chapman now began to appear irregularly. Upon her hard inner gayety must have been heaped exasperation and fatigue. If the stage in California had offered the Chapmans many a lucky chance for adventure, it had been a grueling experience. Theirs had been the lot of the actors who had stayed, weathering every gale of taste or fancy, forced to keep the high pitch of excitement which men massed together after wild turns of fortune inevitably demanded. If they had had full purses flung to make a carpet on the stage they had also been forced to give way before new figures, to take to the mines whether they wished this or not, to adapt, juggle, or invent, to play an interminable variety of pieces in rapid succession. In Sacramento, during one of their brief engagements there, they had offered an immense repertoire, which had included *Julius Caesar, Civilization,* a new play which had had a great vogue abroad, *Hercule, the Huron,* one of the naturalistic pieces of which California audiences seemed to be fond, *Mohammed, Louis XIV,* and an ambitious play apparently patterned after Burton's famous *Mob at the Lyceum,* in which a manager, a prompter, stage-carpenters, actors, lamplighters, appeared in clashes and counter-clashes, giving favored glimpses of episodes behind the scenes, with an amateur actress to the fore whose part was taken by Caroline Chapman. This piece, which perhaps contained more of topical allusion than appeared on the bill, was entitled *First Night; or the Virgin in California.* As if this ambitious production were not enough, the Chapmans tagged it with an opulent afterpiece called *Midas.*

No actors ever gave so abundantly of their talents as the Chapmans; but after their last round in the mines they obviously were approaching the end of their high powers. With unbroken daring they repeated their new burlesque of Lola Montez from time to time, as if even with diminishing houses they were bound to exercise a personal candor and please themselves. But they were on the decline, not only because of their own flagging energy but because they were obliged to meet the massed and solid rivalry of minstrelsy. Presently Caroline Chapman, who had been a brilliant Lady Teazle, who could play an ardent, enchanting Juliet in spite of her high gawky stature and plain appearance and her years, who had at her command a more extensive repertoire than any actress who had appeared on the California stage—the defeated Miss Chapman sought to meet minstrelsy on its own ground, and came out in *Uncle Tom's Cabin* blacked up as Topsy.

Even with this capitulation patronage fell off at the American. The Chapmans receded. Lola Montez, pensively in the ascendant, held assemblies in her iron house in the midst of her many-colored birds. Her circle was now smaller and rather more select than that which she had gathered around her during her first stay in San Francisco or at Grass Valley. The time had gone by when she welcomed any amusing rowdy for momentary diversion. She now studied spiritualism, like many serious minds of the day; there was no doubt about the lowered key of her present existence. But Mrs. Crabtree, who saw her during this interlude, was apparently more aware of the stormy than of the musing strain in Lola's temperament. She declined to let Lotta visit the iron house. Lola talked of taking Lotta with her to Paris, talked so freely and so incessantly that when she came out to the ranch near the Presidio for a visit Mrs. Crabtree hid the child in the barracks, and afterward declared her conviction that Lola had meant to kidnap Lotta.

At last, after a trip to Grass Valley with her white cockatoo on her shoulder, Lola Montez took a final engagement at the Metropolitan under the management of Junius Booth and sailed away in a blaze of recovered glory on the *Orizaba*. The tale came back that on the voyage yellow fever broke out, and that she saved the life of a young lad whom the captain was ready to cast overboard, and nursed him back to health. Tales by the dozen, even the hundred, drifted back to San Francisco about Lola Montez, or found their way over the country. In some fashion this extraordinary woman, whose indubitable personal record is so meager, who at the end was to leave only a combination of hearsay, fable, and a small knot of facts behind her, contrived to keep her name and the print of her character—true or supposed—in the popular mind until she died, and even after.

At the moment of her departure from San Francisco occurred a slight coincidence of time and place. The evening on which she sailed saw small Lotta Crabtree attaining her first appearance at a legitimate theater in San Francisco. This was on a mixed bill at the American, where the Chapmans were still in management. Caroline Chapman appeared in a farce, and sang the popular elegy, *He Died at His Post Doing Duty,* composed at the death of James King of William. There were a few light turns of singing and dancing; then "La Petite Lotta" appeared, thus named on the hanger. The event for the Crabtrees was triumphant. It was achieved too with a sufficient suggestion of local peril, for the night before a man had been shot and killed at the American in a trivial encounter.

Lotta played just one evening. Dr. Robinson strolled into town at this juncture, perhaps in time to witness the performance. The next night Lotta's place was taken by Sue Robinson. Undoubtedly Mrs. Crabtree concluded that warfare was to be an accompaniment of life for herself, for Lotta, as well as for the major theatrical figures. It was a complex struggle. Striking characters, with every element of personality in full accent, these had been plentiful on the California stage, and had borne off the prizes. To an amateur young manager with no guide but her wits, these figures must have loomed again in fabulous proportions, now that she had lost her new slight foothold; and she could hardly have found comfort in the quick decline which had followed so many brilliant ascents.

Young Edwin Booth had departed in the midst of the many cataclysms, receiving two generous benefit performances in Sacramento after his ill fortune in the mines, and another in San Francisco. Many another actor, destined to less fame, had stayed a few years on the Coast and had gone. Most of the vivacious productions of earlier years, those gay burlesques, the operatic extravaganzas, the dar-

ing ballets, even the wealth of Shakespearean performances, had proved fragile. A more experienced critic might
have said that this could not but be so, that in the feverish
haste of new experiment under difficult circumstances, with
the dash and daring required as audiences freely changed,
whatever of charm came into being on the stage must have
been short-lived, and that actors as well as productions
might go down in the maelstrom of fortune. The wonder
was that so much of high excellence had appeared, that so
persistent a progress had been made.

Even in the milling confusion of the theater in 1856
there was still an abundant vitality. That the scene was
full of uncounted possibilities had been proved by the
gala appearances of Julia Dean, a sweet and strange apparition to arrive in San Francisco after the sequence of
stormy characters who had enthralled the public there. No
actress was so surrounded by legend which verged upon
poetry in the mid-century as was Julia Dean. She came of
a family of actors, the famous Drakes. Young as she was
when she traveled to California—she was only in her mid-
twenties—she had achieved an enchanting personal reputation. "Quiet, shy, modest Julia! . . . tall and willowy,
graceful as a swan . . . whose voice was sweet, with the
most tender music in it," mused Joseph Jefferson, who had
played with her in the utility ranks during hard tours in
the South. Such hymns were to be heard abundantly in
New York during the early fifties when she came forward

as a star, playing Julia in *The Hunchback*—her favorite
part—Parthenia in *Ingomar*, Juliet, and the title rôle
in *Griselda*. As she looks out of a delicate old sun-pearl
it is easy to see why she cast so bewitching a spell. She was
not only beautiful, with an air of innocent coquetry; she
was the perfection of the chaste and lovely heroine, appearing now by an odd dispensation against a rough and
tumultuous background.

In San Francisco Julia Dean received a more brilliant
welcome than had been accorded to any actress. She played
at the Metropolitan for thirty nights without a break,
which was then considered an unprecedented run. At
Sacramento she was received with heightened enthusiasm
for an equal period; she returned to San Francisco for
another long engagement, where she gave the initial performance at Maguire's Opera House. For Maguire, taking
a quiet step forward, had transformed the little San Francisco into a larger and more completely equipped theater.

If at the moment Mrs. Crabtree was overwhelmed by
the rise of another dominating figure on the stage she perhaps drew comfort from this new radiance. In time Lotta
might become a famous actress, but she could also be
lovely and good. There was Julia Dean! Oddly enough, a
portrait of Lotta in later years suggests the sun-pearl of
the gentle Julia, by the pose of the head, the demure
glance, the rounded contour of the chin. But there were
differences. Though Lotta was to be good—the fate was

upon her from the beginning—and though she could be demure enough, mischief always rose from her gravity. It did now; her charm as a dancer and small actress lay in the absurd combination of artlessness and the increasing audacity of her tiny acts. She had already learned many a wild flourish of heels from the austere teacher, her mother. The baffling circumstance was that with these unmistakable attractions Lotta was still no further advanced in her new profession than when she had first gone on at the Bella Union.

In the growing lusty life of the city openings should have been plentiful. Entertainment was growing apace. The Russ Gardens and Hayes Park were now places of diversion, with spacious promenades and little tables set out doors in the continental style. Here were balloon ascensions; and many small acts were produced. Scarcely a popular house of refreshment failed to offer singing and dancing when crowds were gathered. On Long Wharf, now a fashionable promenade, was a famous resort which even the most fastidious ladies might invade, which indeed wore a special air of innocence with its Bath buns and jellies, its mutton pies and sweets of clove, boneset, mint, or sassafras, and a sprinkling of Scotch buds and sugar-plums. Here, too, was entertainment. A minstrel gave blackface acts with a song and dance in the midst of lavish repasts. But for Lotta there seemed only the chance to munch an occasional sweet in this place, and watch the swishing of skirts and the toss of feathered hats, or to mingle with crowds on her mother's arm as they trudged about looking for new openings.

There were plenty of things for a child to see on such journeyings: the peddlers of charcoal, the trail of the water-wagon in long curves over wooden planking, bits of odd life which flourished in pit-like basements along the streets. But such diversions for an inquisitive small mind were hardly a reason for lingering in San Francisco. A decision had to be made as spring drew on, which for Mrs. Crabtree became infinitely difficult. Crabtree had come to the city, at last discovering the whereabouts of his family. His wife was convinced that he meant to take Lotta from her. As when she became aware of the intense interest of Lola Montez, she hid the child in the Presidio.

Perhaps each time Mrs. Crabtree was the victim of a passionate, disturbed fancy. Beset by novel forces, she hardly knew which way to turn. What arrangement was made at last is not clear, but some kind of truce in the family was finally reached. Handsomer and more able-bodied than ever, Crabtree continued to float in and out of the lives of his wife and daughter for years, always well-dressed—increasingly so as Lotta's triumphs became marked—claiming from his wife a reluctant toleration, even an illogical pride. At least in one direction her difficulties now diminished. Her twin sister Charlotte had come to San Francisco. Mrs. Crabtree was able to leave

the two small boys in her care when, in the spring of
1857, she decided to travel again with Lotta in the mountains.

Once more she joined forces with Mart Taylor, who
still wore his jetty long curls, and who now had published
his own song-book, and had gained a considerable repute
in the mountains as a poet. Mrs. Crabtree was again to
play the triangle, and under the name of Miss Arabella to
give occasional impersonations. There were a few other
musicians in the small troupe. Borrowing luster, they
called themselves the Metropolitan Company, and set out,
up the Sacramento as before, and over the wide floor of
the valley northward.

In the clear mountain air, as they traveled past blue
meadows of mountain iris, the journey had the aspect of a
holiday. Stage-coach drivers were inveterate jokers. On
steep grades the whole company would dismount, and the
men would help push the laden coach up the mountain-
side. There was always the tang of danger; all coaches
carried treasure boxes laden with money, or on the downward journey gold dust; robberies were common, and
highwaymen had an effective way of lassoing travelers
who scurried off through the brush to sound an alarm. The
mountains were full of mysterious, threatening characters.
Commonly enough, a pair of well-armed visitors would
be described in a hotel register by the laconic phrase "Two
Strangers." But the risk of robbery was not too great; the

little Metropolitan Company was now traveling through fairly well-frequented regions along the great lode. Special threats and obstacles came from another quarter.

The new journey of the Crabtrees was far different from that which they had undertaken two summers before in the high Sierras. In these more settled regions the time had passed when women were received with ardent curiosity or excited gallantry; nor were children now objects of special sentiment. Too many of them had skipped through the mining camps with inconsiderable talent, presuming upon tender hearts. An intense competition had begun in mountain theatricals. Many ambitious companies were crowding over the trails, often pulling up with wagon and drum at a camp only a few yards ahead of another band, each hopeful of securing the only available theater. Half a dozen minstrel troupes were on their way from San Francisco. Wagon shows, freely borrowing the names of well-known actors, were roaming over the mountains, offering wench dances, a burlesque circus, an Ethiopian act, with a calico party for conclusion. Small circuses were struggling into the mountains with a bit of property, a wild animal or two, a few acrobats. As the season advanced nearly all the well-known players of the San Francisco stage appeared in the larger camps. One company traveled more than a thousand miles on foot and on horseback, playing at a different camp each night.

With so ample a display mountain audiences were growing captious. In the steady cycle of plays in the cities and in the mines there had been many repetitions; the miners knew the popular dramas almost by heart, could finish lines from Shakespeare before they were spoken; they had played at amateur theatricals: they were versed in the theater. They protested that they did not care to see well-worn plays like *The Lady of Lyons*. They often tossed displeasing actors in blankets. A cracking shot was likely to dust the heels of an unlucky performer as he left town.

A company of three young boys who crossed the track of the Metropolitan Company was met by raucous laughter as they entered one camp. They persisted in making ready for their entertainment, pasted up the cracks in a rough little dressing-room with newspapers, stuck candles in bottles in front of the stage, and faced the leveled revolver of the bully of the camp. In a tremolo that was not altogether histrionic they proclaimed that they were only three boys, that they had come to give a show not to fight: in increasingly shaky tones they announced their conviction that two hundred armed men would not harm them. The tremolo wailed and broke. The bully likewise wept, as promptly and copiously as though he had been playing melodrama. After the entertainment the miners spread an excellent supper for the trio, and sent them on their way with a tin mustard box full of gold nuggets. But George Chapman and his family, who had traveled through the mountains repeatedly since 1851, had finally bored the

From a miniature in the collection of John S. Drum

LOLA MONTEZ

JULIA DEAN

miners, though they were not unaccomplished players. They had received repeated warnings, and were now on their way northward over rough corduroy roads in a wagon toward Oregon, hoping for less sensitive audiences and more leisurely gestures in the direction of hip-pockets.

Solemnity was the miners' watchword when McKean Buchanan played—solemnity with unbridled enthusiasm. Buchanan was likely to create a Macbeth who strode on to the stage amid blue fire in a slouch hat with a great drooping feather, a long black cape, arms folded high, ominously patting one arm with a huge yellow gauntlet, stepping across the stage with heel methodically brought to heel, each time with a deep pause. Bound together as by a pact, the somber miners saluted such scenes with cannonades of applause. Gaining an enormous momentum, Buchanan knocked Bosworth Field to pieces, shouted himself hoarse as Richelieu, died again and again with heaving, pounding reluctance, or at the end of any play was likely to sweep about in a mazy circle which some wag called a walk-around, and was said to devour portions of the scenery. At Calaveras Grove, by concerted action, no suitable stage could be found for Buchanan, and he was coaxed into the novelty of playing on the stump of a large redwood tree, with an outcome on which the audience, looking toward further diversion of the same kind, was silent. Indeed Buchanan was liked in the mountains, not only for the entertainment which he provided, but for his integrity, and because he was an accomplished gambler. When an evening's production failed to yield enough to pay his company, he went out after the play and won enough at poker to settle his bills the next morning.

"Go roll a prairie up like cloth,
    Drink Mississippi dry,
Put Allegheny in your hat,
    A steamboat in your eye—
And for your breakfast buffalo
    Some five and twenty fry.

"Go kill the whole Comanche tribe,
    Some day before you dine;
Pick out to make your walking-stick
    A California pine;
And then turn round and frown so dark
    The sun won't dare to shine.

"Go whip a ton of grizzly bears
    With nothing but a tan;
And prove yourself by all these feats
    To be a western man,
And you can write a poem grand
    If anybody can."

Such satirical magniloquence, breaking forth in mining camp papers, was abroad in a dozen forms. Irresponsibility was at large, bringing crime, blackness, despair, and also gayety, freshness, the springs of new existence. Footloose, this new population set free a shattering fun and made its own standards, and—for the terror of players like the new and humble Metropolitan Company—had its own extensive repertoire. Scattered all through the mountains, the miners were nothing less than a huge variety troupe, practiced not only in dramatic forms or the rude histrionics of the practical joke, but most of all in songs, or for that matter even in dances. They had at once drifted into fandangos, were critical of waltz forms, had watched intensely all the elaborate solo steps. But songs were their pride and possession.

According to usual notions, encouraged in part by the miners themselves, they should have sung about distant homes and firesides. It is true that they picturesquely represented themselves in the midst of reveries on this theme. The miner's dream—the miner recumbent, the dream of home floating in the air—appeared on the drop-curtains of many mountain theaters and on at least one in San Francisco, and was repeated on favorite broadsides. But the subject was not conspicuous in current songs; nor were the sentimental lyrics of the time, *Belle Brandon*, *Sweet Annie of the Vale*, and their like, overwhelmingly popular, though they were sung. The tearful sentimental heroine had never been a dominant figure on the California stage, even though hardened miners were supposed to melt like wax when such creatures appeared in life or in literature or on the stage.

On the contrary, through a wild fun ran an odd vein of realism in this vagrant self-expression. The miners were incurably interested in themselves. Almost from the first months of the gold rush, writing to sedate distant correspondents, they had used great sheets of letter paper on which were lithographed scenes of mountain life, not in utopian forms, but in the close rough view: pictures of huddled camps, gambling houses, dance-halls, interiors of rude cabins. They liked to display themselves at their unlikely tasks of cooking and mending, in the midst of the elaborate hard work of digging tunnels, making flumes, washing gold. With an ostentatious bid for sympathy, broadsides with pictures and verses were sent home which spelled out the sequence of the miner's day, or revealed his toils and troubles.

In song they kept a wild, audacious key. Hardly a circumstance which belonged to mining life had failed to find an outlet in a bold ballad. A whole epic had been built up around the Pike County emigration. Tall men, awkward, melancholy, suspicious, wearing tight, high-waisted surtouts that belonged to the eighteenth century, and cloth suspenders, these odd invaders were the remnant of some early immigration which had ventured into the Mississippi Valley. Some of them had never seen a village. But they could use their long-barreled rifles with deadly swiftness. The pastime of putting them into satirical verse could hardly have been a holiday affair. Yet there they were—these Missourians—imprisoned like the Chinese in a dozen long-winded, laconic musical narratives. Nothing escaped the tuneful miners. They composed radical satires on their expectations of fortune. They put Sam Brannan into verse—"He once was a great Mormon." They burst into vituperation over the panic—

"They agreed among themselves they could easy make a
    pile,
  By stealing all they had on deposit—"

They sang simple songs about the mud in San Francisco—

"In wand'ring round a man I found,
  With sounding lead and grappling gear—"

and other admiring ones about "our city," its mixture of peoples, its perpetual haste, its dominant figures—

"Gentlemanly gambler,
  Wealthy city broker,
Taking brandy smashes,
  And a game of poker;
Gambler very cool,
  Broker very dry,
Stocks are getting *low*,
  Broker getting *high!*

"Steamers leave today
　　For Atlantic States,
　Great excitement *raised*
　　By *reducing* rates—
　Miners in red shirts
　　Shooting home like rockets,
　Bags of yellow dust
　　Lining ragged pockets."

A murderous song about ship owners was bellowed forth after the loss of the *Central America*. To the air of *Walk Ye In* another ballad celebrated the *Steam Navigation Thieves*—

"The only legal swindle which the people cannot sever
　Is the steamboat imposition on the Sacramento River—

Refrain:

　"Keep your hands upon your money,
　　Or they'll rob you on the way."

An equally bitter onslaught was made on the California Stage Company—

　"They started as a thieving line,
　　In eighteen hundred forty-nine . . ."

The miners chattered endlessly in song about fleas, scurvy, rain, weevilly biscuits, all the trials of the voyage out, the plague of fever, the cruelty of captains, the sad fate of the "dying Californian," a legendary youth who continued to captivate the fancy of these singers for many years. They likewise shouted in stentorian chorus—

"Then hurra! hurra! for our pine-clad hills,
Where the ruddy miner works by the gushing rills,
He knows no cares—he knows no ills,
But laughs ha! ha! ha! ha! as his purse he fills."

"If any of the sojourners in the mountains, while breathing the pure air, and contemplating nature from the lofty Sierra Nevada, feels kindle the spark of enthusiasm in praise of his country, please send the poems along," begged the editor of one of the many California songbooks. Massett had celebrated the Yuba River in verse and song. An unknown writer had tried to ensnare the wild beauty of the country about Nevada City in awkward verses. But a rough satirical balance was kept.

A strong undercurrent of veracity ran through these ballads, appearing in the racy narrative of a California "ball" or in *The California Widow*, which was packed with lively puns. If a rude lyricism was abroad there were also plentiful *Miner's Laments*, some of them built on the favorite subject of the *Miner's Dream*—with an abrupt awakening—others rough and realistic throughout. At times whole companies would troll out the mellifluous *To the West! To the West!—*

"To the West! to the West! Where the rivers that flow
Run thousands of miles, spreading out as they go;
Where the green waving forests shall echo our call,
As wide as old England, and free to us all!
Where the prairies like seas, where the billows have
    rolled,
Are broad as the kingdoms and empires of old,
And the lakes are like oceans, in storm or in rest,
Away, far away, to the land of the West!"

Then with gusto would come the counter-song of the
same name, which proclaimed that the West had robbed
the singers of their last hopes and illusions, or the bitter
little *California over the Left,* or *When I Went Off to
Prospect,* or *The Fools of Forty-nine.*

This was the formidable public which confronted the
new Metropolitan Company. One of Lotta's companions
attracted the adverse attention of a truculent miner who
grazed him with a shot. The actor fled from the camp
without a word and was never heard from again. The
company was often obliged to play in tents; and probably
no troupe ever passed a season without having a tent blown
away by high winds or ripped from its moorings by
practical jokers. But the continual test was in the audience
hall. An alert adjustment, something more than hair-
trigger wariness, was everywhere. In the midst of that

electric contagion almost any actor might lose his balance and fall headlong into hysteria or futility. Every one who appeared was obliged to maintain a high and fluent intensity, and to match the level of entertainment which the miners themselves could provide.

But it was not for nothing that Mrs. Crabtree had lived at Grass Valley and Rabbit Creek, and had traveled through the mountains on that first tense trip. If the mood of a miners' audience was constantly changing, if a year in this period was equivalent to a decade in more stolid times, so that no experience was ever quite a preparation, still she had learned the essential character of the people and the place, and had a temper which was both implacable and adaptive to match it. She could keep Lotta in high equable key: and the child herself seemed to have caught an essential note. She could stand in the middle of a tiny stage and laugh, and a whole roomful of miners would join in an uproar. From that high-pitched response she seemed to gain power, even freedom, and an increasing momentum. "The singing and dancing of little Lotta was admirable, and took our hearts by storm," said a notice in a mining paper at Forest City, where the company played in a little upstairs theater. She kept her head high above the ordinary entertainment and flung out to those mixed assemblages a comedy that was all but tangible. Her odd and innocent boldness raced with something articulate in her

audience; and besides a small repertoire of the miners'
songs about themselves, she had caught the favorite burlesque patterns of minstrelsy.

On the way up from Sacramento the company had
stopped at Placerville, where Mart Taylor had found a
negro breakdown dancer of considerable skill who was
willing to teach Lotta a vigorous and complicated soft-
shoe dancing. Along the trail the Taylor troupe had combined for a night or two with Backus's minstrels, long since
entrenched in San Francisco and a highly favored company
in the mountains. Some one suggested that Lotta black up
and sing a Topsy song—

> "I can play the banjo, yes, indeed I can!
> I can play a tune upon the frying pan,
> I hollo like a steamboat 'fore she's gwine to stop,
> I can sweep a chimney and sing out at the top—"

Gone forever seemed the hope of legitimate theatricals
for Lotta. In San Francisco, passing the smaller halls,
from the air itself she might have caught the essence of
minstrelsy. She liked it. A breakdown number became
inevitable on her bill. She romped and sang and lustily
danced in blackface, and at the end of her numbers when
the stage was covered with money and nuggets, kicked off
a shoe and ran about filling it with dollars and gold slugs,
obviously a child who had forgotten her part for a moment
and was pleased with her rewards. She added many of

the minstrel songs of the day to her numbers. The old
Sich a Gittin' Upstairs was still popular, *Jim Along Josie*,
the *Long Tail Blue*, and an infinite number of miners'
variations on *O Susanna!* which had now begun to show
a reversion toward the underlying minstrel strain. Some of
these songs called for a buck and wing—

"Trike de toe and heel, cut de pigeon wing,
Scratch gravel, slap de foot, dat's jus' de ting—"

Lotta could touch off the highly masculine steps in tiny
miniature, with a quick, grotesque little rhythm.

She still laughed when she danced. Few dancers, old
or young, could now match her repertoire of steps. In her
tiny long-tailed green coat she danced her Irish jigs and
reels. She sang Cockney songs like *I'm the Covey What
Sings* with pantomime, or the nautical *My Mary Ann*—

"A lobster in a lobster pot,
A bluefish wriggling on a hook,
May suffer some, but oh! no! not
What I do feel for my Mary Ann—"

The ridiculous ballad came to life because she could mimic
a bumpkin sailor, and follow the song with a hornpipe.
She sang sentimental songs in white cambric less frequently than on her first tour, though one or two of these,
if sufficiently popular at the moment, seemed to please her
audiences by way of contrast. But she was soon back in

blackface again on the same bill, constantly adding new pantomime to her parts with the assistance of Taylor and her mother, or by her own ingenuity and spontaneous action. Even the matter of picking up money and nuggets she turned into comic business. She would come out with an old hat held at a rakish angle on her elbow, create a bit of comedy by her glances at the gold pieces, and another by putting them into the hat, which had no bottom. Through this long summer she acquired an ample stock of comic pantomime, and learned to give her small acts something of rounded finish and completion.

Mrs. Crabtree's skill was taxed to the utmost, as she contrived costumes, played the triangle, made up Lotta in blackface with a quick change, and maintained that invisible barrier which was part of her assurance that her choice for the child had been a right one. Severe and upright, still a handsome woman with her high color and fine eyes, Mrs. Crabtree also appeared on the stage occasionally, and as Miss Arabella won her share of applause and ringing half dollars. What her impersonations were cannot be learned at this distance: to judge from others of the same time, these were burlesques of actresses conspicuous on the San Francisco stage. One would guess that Mrs. Crabtree gave her caricatures fearlessly and fluently, with a touch of acid. No one was afraid of bold acting in those days; and the whilom Miss Arabella, who had be-

come deeply aware of stage rivalries, would certainly have
let her own hard humor have full play.

During brief interludes the whole company threw off
responsibility and entertained each other instead of an
exacting audience. In the give and take of travel Mrs.
Crabtree had a knack of surface companionship, though
at bottom this usual human drift seemed to concern her
very little. As a rule when an evening's entertainment was
over the whole troupe would quickly make its way out of
the rear door of the hall or theater to waiting horses,
would mount and be off along a dark trail. Lotta, dressed
in boy's clothes, slept at night on horseback as before she
had slept riding a mule, with the halter held by a rider in
front. Bowlders frequently crashed down across the trails,
loosened by continual mining operations. Trees snapped
and fell. A few times in early daylight, as she afterwards
remembered, Lotta saw a lone rider far ahead slip and
plunge down a ravine. On into a new camp they would
ride, after a brief rest, with Taylor beating the drum;
then more rest, and the night's performance. Scarcely a
player who rode the trails in these years failed later to
look back with pleasure to the experience; and the Crabtrees were no exception. They talked about it; Mrs. Crabtree unrolled her great knapsack of observation; but if
Lotta often spoke of sleeping peacefully on horseback
her mother seldom mentioned a similar circumstance for

herself. Perhaps during these long night journeys Mrs. Crabtree rode wide awake.

They traveled far up into the high Sierras through the summer and autumn along little-known trails, until snow fell in a sudden deep carpet; then they dipped again, riding in coaches through rainy weather to the lower towns. The season had been prosperous. Comfortable and secure, the Crabtrees returned to San Francisco in the early winter, with every prospect of a new success. Lotta was now favorably known all through the mountains to the north and down the lode toward Calaveras. She had a genuine following among the miners who constantly drifted down the rivers to the larger towns. With her new blackface numbers and the season's steady training she was ready to plunge into the high theatrical business of the moment, that of minstrelsy. Again, under the silent, ardent patronage of Maguire, minstrelsy was well to the fore; nearly every other form of theatrical enterprise had been blotted out.

Perhaps Lotta's turns were what they were later claimed to be, a genuine novelty in minstrelsy. But Maguire, bent upon a startling combination of the better-known blackface players, was not interested in Lotta. It was rumored that he spoke slightingly of her talents. At this moment Crabtree stepped forward, possibly with a recollection of the valiant father of the Bateman children who had shot a critic. With a small revolver Crabtree winged Maguire in the Square. The damage was slight, a mere flick of a bullet. Maguire, with his usual calm, seems to have sauntered away, but whether he buried the memory like many others, or kept the grudge, can never be told. Lotta was to remain in San Francisco theatricals, and so was Maguire. Some time later they made an alliance, though this was never firm; and it is possible that Crabtree's bullet, like his wife's silent passage at arms with Dr. Robinson at Rabbit Creek, had its effect upon Lotta's career.

At least Crabtree won a new prestige; and finally, out of the ruck of obscure possibilities, Lotta was given an engagement at a small theater called the Gaieties, a "bit" theater, a shabby place on the waterfront surrounded by a dumping ground, junk shops, cheap clothing houses, low groggeries. This tiny hall, with an entrance through a bar-room, was a narrow place upstairs, around three sides of which ran an overhanging gallery. In front of the little stage, lit by a row of tallow dips, were a few groups of tables around which the actors usually sat awaiting their turns, for they were obliged to enter through the house, and there were only two small dressing-rooms. The manager of the Gaieties was Rowena Granice, the players professionals out of luck, a few amateurs, a few circus performers. The theater was patronized mainly by miners down from the mountains, one of whom wrote an account of a performance there.

The play of the evening was *Brigham Young*, with the

title rôle taken by an acrobat. His "sultana" was the "ripe-aged Miss Rowena." Three juveniles played the other wives. The audience was in a wild mood on this occasion, and offered a quick staccato of advice and rowdy remarks throughout the play. As Miss Rowena prepared to slay the roving prophet the miners howled, and howled again when the acrobatic Brigham, having answered in tones of high tragedy, was obliged to abandon this effect, turn super, and blow out the candles in order to create the proper darkness for a dream. When at last he was settled in a reclining position as the dreaming prophet, the ghost of a murdered wife appeared. Unfortunately at this moment the three juveniles, by this time wholly out of their rôles as wives, came forward with bits of low comedy and successfully continued their antics until the room shook with laughter, and the clouds of tobacco smoke waved like curtains.

After the play Lotta came on with *Shells of the Ocean*—

> "One summer eve, with pensive thought,
>   I wandered on the sea-beat shore,
>   Where oft, in heedless infant sport,
>   I gathered shells in days before."

But she was hoarse and broke down. She persisted in trying to pick up the air. The miners, many of whom had known her in the mountains, called to her in encourage-

LOTTA. ABOUT 1858

DOWNIEVILLE

ment, but her warm temper broke forth as she failed, and at last she ran off in a hasty pet like an untried little girl who had never before been on a stage. The candles were now burning blue through the smoke. The drinking throng was growing boisterous. A fight was on the way. Mrs. Crabtree, shielding Lotta, made her way out through the single exit.

They must have made many such exits, watched many such performances as they awaited Lotta's turn. Calculate as she might, Mrs. Crabtree could hardly whisk Lotta into her part precisely on the moment. But the engagement at the Gaieties was brief. Early in 1858 Rowena Granice was playing in Sacramento with a Yankee comedian who had once been the head of a large Mormon colony. Poor Miss Granice seemed as deeply intrigued by Mormons in life as in art; she married the comedian, who proved a hopeless rover. But drab and battered as she had become, there was a sturdy strain in Rowena Granice, and a kind one. Through her, Lotta seems to have obtained an engagement at the Forrest Theatre in Sacramento. She came out in a burletta, and had her brief moment as a rising small star. Unfortunately she assumed the title, and was announced on the hangers as the "Fairy Star." More than any other young actress Sue Robinson had won the name; and she was soon back in Sacramento after a tour of the mines. Lotta was withdrawn.

As summer came on nothing was offered Lotta except

another journey through the mines, this time southward. From Stockton over the wide San Joaquin Valley the Crabtrees set out again by coach late in 1858, past deep tulé marshes, moist and copper-green in winter, now afire. Flocks of magpies arose, and tufted partridges. Many seekers of luck were afloat in the valley. Again the Crabtrees were weaving their way among other actors. Julia Dean had recently been playing in Mariposa, with Frank Mayo, genial Walter Leman, and others, in a barn without a floor where the miners brought stools and staked off places like claims. On one occasion this company, playing upstairs in a tiny cloth and paper house, had been obliged to use two narrow windows for exits and entrances. One troupe had seen its trunkful of costumes, unlashed from a stagecoach, pitch down a steep ravine to split upon rocks below and scatter into a tumbling stream.

There were tales of the ubiquitous John S. Potter, already known in the mining newspapers as the Micawber of the California stage, the man "who had built more theaters and opened more theaters—I think he closed twice as many as he ever opened—than any man in the Union or out of it," said one of his companions. He was always persuading good actors to join him. Mrs. Judah, Sophie Edwin, and others among the strong and staple players of the time had traveled under his management. "What, ask for salaries when blackberries are ripe!" he would reproachfully ask one of the company who begged for a dollar or two of back salary. Assuming any part on ten minutes' notice in a black cloak and wig, shifting scenes, arranging properties, within a few moments after the final curtain Potter would be off and out of the sight of his company with the box office receipts in his pocket.

Perhaps Mrs. Crabtree was fortunate in her choice of company; perhaps not. Her companions are unknown; the whole venture is shrouded in obscurity. The company of which she was a part must have traveled through the smaller camps, for little or no trace of their tour remains. If they went as far south as Mariposa they experienced once more something of that idyllic quality which had met them in spring in the north, finding now a deep golden idyll in summer when the hillsides grew lemon-yellow, brown, and copper-color, the black oaks tawny. Everywhere whirled a velvet ocher dust. Through sequoias and high sugar pines they must have hurried over rough mountain roads, perhaps catching a sudden flitter of indigo as blue-jays rose with a wide spread of wing and sooty crests. Even that transcendent color was veiled. In summer dust was a palpable atmosphere on these roads, arising in clouds, yellow or rose or whitey-gray according to the soil, settling upon pine and cypress and manzanita until these looked like strange antediluvian growths with thickened leaves and stiffly contorted branches.

In the tangible haze everything was magnified. A miner, pausing with uplifted pick, would have seen the high stage-coach lurching by in a deep swirling envelope of dust, horses and coach looking far greater than their size, the spokes of wheels catching the hot light, the whole train a ghost, looking as though it might dissolve in the deeper clouds of dust beyond. Cool spaces sometimes caught the eye where lupine grew in wet grassy valleys, small as jewels within the rising heights of the Sierras, and quickly gone.

The Crabtrees perhaps paused at Mormon Bar, sunk in dry heat across a river-bed. They may have climbed to the shallow cup which held Mariposa, and played at Hornitos, the wildest of all camps in the southern mines, which possessed a hard and bitter legend of lynchings and of orgiastic fandangos. Everywhere were the same cloth and paper houses, the same insistent audience, the same hilarious fun. Sometimes a theater would go up in flames and smoke before they arrived. Whole villages were quickly caught in a cloud of fire. Still they traveled, perhaps over the steep mountain road which led to Big Oak Flat, traversing the streaked copper-pink hills by perilous grades, through Priest's, Moccasin Creek, Chinese Camp. If, as seems likely, they played through the Calaveras camps on the way out, it would have been toward autumn when they reached these great descents after the long loop southward. Rains would be setting in; and though these were welcome to lay the dust, they created the breath-taking dangers of slippery roads and high rivers. The Tuolumne, often a rushing torrent even in mid-summer, grew to a flood which tore away ferries in early winter.

Sonora may have seemed a welcome haven. Still a rough mining camp, the little village had already taken on a delicate contour, as though the print of some distant tradition were shaping uncouth materials. Lying easily within the sloping outline of low hills, the town kept its plaza; the rising street had a pleasant turn; a few houses of dignity with spacious dooryards had been built along its narrow curve; a spire rose at the crest. Hawthorne had been planted, pomegranates, crêpe myrtle, and bay, with hedges of box. Mrs. Crabtree might have found there a memory of English lanes. Yet the traces that Lotta played in Sonora are faint. Perhaps one of those passages of ill luck which befell many actors now befell the Crabtrees. They may have arrived on the heels of a rival attraction. In any case they could not have paused for more than a day or two.

Through all that journey, as they traveled onward, Mrs. Crabtree must have been stirred by a profound discouragement. Was there nothing ahead but traveling in the mines? Over and again Lotta had come to the surface of the larger theatrical scene only to be thrust relentlessly aside. Perhaps it was part of this unaccountable profession to bob to the surface and disappear, just as actors came out for a time in the glare of kerosene lamps and dropped again into the blackness of night. Hardly philosophical, readier far for action or decision, she had plenty of time to ponder such questions: but her first purpose seems not to have wavered. She was returning with Lotta to San Francisco, bent upon securing engagements.

Gathering what returns they could, following their exacting routine, they worked their way back along main trails. The hillsides were emerald now, the madrones brilliant with orange berries; if they experienced rain and sleet there were plenty of days with a providentially blue sky overhead. Perhaps they spent Christmas in camp, as many players did, as the Crabtrees seem to have done at least once—almost surely now—with a tree on the stage, and trimmings of manzanita in pearly bloom, its tiny bells and purple-brown stems gay as tinsel. This was an up-roarious and generous time, the miners giving lavishly of gold, the players of their stored repertoire. One can fancy Lotta, at a high pitch of excitement—more child than player—dancing out, as a small black Sambo, or again in her white frock to sing with her red curls flying. Then out they traveled once more, through fantastic chaparral, pale and grotesque and leafless, over the plain to Stockton, and returned to San Francisco at last by river-boat on the San Joaquin, mingling with miners down for a winter's holiday.

V

THE WILD HORSE OF TARTARY

A PAGE HAD BEEN TURNED IN SAN FRANCISCO THEATRI-
cals when the Crabtrees arrived there early in 1859. The
drama had almost vanished, drawing into obscurity many
of the major figures that had given it brilliance. Variety
—not yet called vaudeville—had come into an overwhelming popularity.

At the end of the fifties a whole galaxy of small halls
sprang into existence in San Francisco, upstairs and below-
stairs, newly built as tiny melodeons or transformed from
small theaters into variety houses. The Bella Union had
now abandoned gambling for variety. Rowena Granice had
gathered a minstrel and variety troupe at the small Union
Theatre. The What Cheer Melodeon soon opened, Gilbert's, a new Athenaeum, a New Mammoth Melodeon,
Sam Wells' Opera House, Tucker's, the Long Tom, the
Jenny Lind. There was now a diminutive stage at the
Willows. Though Maguire had dabbled at intervals in
opera, variety troupes had occupied his boards almost
steadily for several years; and he quickly built the Eureka
Minstrel Hall.

A restless public on the Coast seemed to have rifled the
rich offerings of a decade, and to have flung them aside.

Witty, highly rowdy, creating its own entertainment in
the mines with a profusion of bold songs, masquerades,
and grotesque fandangos, this public now demanded theatricals which were both primitive and complex. Its mood
was ripe for variety. Encounters were still desperate in
California, changes in luck overwhelming, suicides so common that few remarked them, life both amply lived and
cheap. Fantasy, bold rhythm, a smacking wit, above all,
change, had grown increasingly welcome. The miners'
knowledge of theater and of opera, if now apparently
flung away, was still rich. They could watch a blackface
Mr. Othello with half a dozen excellent productions of
Shakespeare in recent memory, could roar at blackface
travesties of *The Bohemian Girl* or *Somnambula,* knowing
the arias and the original groundwork of drama. In this
audience many artificial distinctions had been leveled;
and that by-blow of the theater, variety, dealt with the
common levels of life in all directions, stressing street
characters, country characters, the odd side, the down side,
the rebellious side, introducing the Yankee, the Irish immigrant, and most frequently the negro.

Elsewhere variety had often crept underground, for
in other places the life of the theater was still caught in
a struggle for recognition. On the Coast that struggle had
never existed. The mixed bill had had a continuous growth
there on a level with other entertainment, subject only to
whirlwinds of popular taste.

Irony could be found in the altered scene, heavily smiting a figure which Mrs. Crabtree had reason to consider, that of the small and spirited Dr. Robinson. In San Francisco variety had first crystallized in the topical songs, dances, and burlesques at his little hall with its garish monotone of yellow, when the year of '49 was hardly over. At his later Dramatic Museum and in his lengthening *entr'actes* at the San Francisco Theatre, Dr. Robinson had promoted the same untrammeled entertainment. But at the San Francisco he had at last produced a play of his own called *The Past, Present, and Future of California*, which he had intended as a historical panorama in the grand style, and which had gained a special luster by the appearance of Captain Sutter in the cast, who peaceably consented to impersonate himself. Perhaps Dr. Robinson was carried away by his own wit: but that wit seemed to be swayed by the demand of a thriving public. The serious aspects of his drama had quickly vanished; the piece had grown lighter and lighter. He had added topical allusions, with a burlesque on the subject of women's rights; he introduced a boy into the slender action who had accidentally gone up in a balloon and had floated over the bay. Finally a small black Sambo rolling about had become a portent of the minstrel company by which Dr. Robinson was displaced at Maguire's theater.

But he had tenaciously clung to the original plan for his dramatic panorama: its serious production proved to be the one great wish of his life. He determined to take it to the Atlantic States, but he had fallen a prey to ship's fever on the voyage, and had died at Mobile before he could try his fortunes. Dr. Robinson's panorama was destined never to be produced.

The Chapmans too were lost in the midst of the growing noise and momentum. Playing a minor engagement, William Chapman had died in 1857, looking so old and worn that he was taken for a man of seventy though he was fully fifteen years younger. Caroline Chapman had gone to New York, hoping for engagements which she was not to find; she was to return to San Francisco to face obscurity and illness, occasionally playing a minor part at a benefit or in a small production. During the Civil War something of her old audacity was mirrored in the dash from the bay of a gun-running Confederate brig named in her honor, the *Caroline Chapman;* but this brief flare of rebellion was a slight substitution for the rich family and theatrical life in which she had had a brilliant share for so many years; and the reversal ran the deeper because of her own grasp of the new free modes of acting now apparent on the stage. She too had given an impetus to the lawless theatricals which were culminating in variety.

The change was ruthless. Many a minor actor had been swept aside. Many of the more gifted players who had been on the Coast for years, Mrs. Judah, Sophie Edwin,

Junius Booth, Sue Robinson—who had moved on to the legitimate stage—were taking casual parts in minor performances. Biscaccianti, who had been the first opera singer of high quality to appear in San Francisco, was now singing in variety halls, saluted by sailors with a toss of hats, her lovely voice, a cool coloratura, floating out in one small melodeon after another. A few opera troupes of excellence still came to the Coast under the marshaling leadership of Maguire: from the first, opera and minstrelsy had flourished together. But that exodus of conspicuous figures from the East to the Coast which had given high color to the earlier theatricals had abruptly stopped. Jefferson appeared in San Francisco in 1861. He thought that his failure there came from the circumstance that he was over-billed: but the likelier surmise is that the theater-going public was still uninterested in plays.

Few audiences were so homogeneous; few made evident their desires with such unmistakable power. The variety players too were an intimate band; many of them had been on the Coast from the early years, training in the hard school of the Sierras, most of them in blackface. Minstrelsy was enveloping the usual variety bill—

> "Uncle Gabriel play de fiddle,
> Zip Coon he made de riddle,
> Bone Squash in de middle,
> And dis nigger play de bones,

While de banjo and triangle
With de cymbals jingle jangle,
And de big drum neat we handle—"

The new formula of the first and second "part" with a grand olio and concluding farce was growing in favor. Within this were hospitably sheltered Yankee dialogues, Irish sketches, operatic burlesques, sometimes in blackface, sometimes in full character, and even operatic scenes. The whole force of the theater was there, broken into bold parts against a background of song and dance.

Into this jangling compact world small Lotta Crabtree entered almost at once. With the full flare of variety on the San Francisco stage she came at last into her own. Her career was fixed, not only for immediate engagements but for later years. Whatever Lotta became, however often she was to command plays of her own, she remained essentially a variety actress, with the vivacious original turns, the irrepressible humor, the unaccountable mode of the lighter theater flowing through her chosen parts. Her type of acting had been fixed once and for all by her encounters with mountain audiences, her skill created there. Half a dozen doors were opened to her in the variety houses, though a highly masculine minstrelsy continued to dominate their bills. Maguire, forgetting the affair of Crabtree and his pistol in the Square, took her into the mixed minstrels at his Opera House and at the

Eureka, and gave her a piano as a token of esteem. She played at the What Cheer, Gilbert's, the Willows, the Apollo, the Bella Union. She was now suddenly Miss Lotta, "La Petite Lotta, the Celebrated Danseuse and Vocalist," "Miss Lotta, the Unapproachable," "Miss Lotta, the San Francisco Favorite." The slight dignity was unique on contemporary bills. The few other youthful actresses who gained the variety stage were called "Little Jennie," or merely Lizzie Smith.

If an exacting public wanted diversity, in the small person of Miss Lotta that quality was oddly comprised. She was both sturdy and delicate, full of rowdy caprice and quaintly aloof. Her voice was developing into a flexible soprano with a mezzo range. All her life she was to speak and sing with a smothered fire that seemed at variance with the light content of her words. Her clear tones, which made every syllable carry into the furthest corner of an audience hall, suggested a greater force and more ample meaning than anything she had to say. With *Belle Brandon* on the hanger she would come out, poised and pathetic and sweet, in the mood of the ballad, and then troll out a parody: the name now belonged not only to the birdling of the mountain but to a steamboat on the Sacramento and a new locomotive. With an easy melancholy she would prolong a lawless little ballad called *Chaff and Wink Your Eye.* But it was her dancing, well caught within pantomime and impersonation, which

aroused the special heady enthusiasm which was to en-
velop her for years. Jigs, flings, wild polkas, breakdowns,
the whole range of soft-shoe dancing: in her five or six
years of traveling in the mines or playing to small audiences in San Francisco she had picked up every bold and
lively changing step which could provoke a sudden cheer,
and danced them with a delicate sprightliness or a rough
and romping humor. Her dancing was light as gossamer
when she wished it to be, or boldly hoydenish. She danced
as Topsy, as a wild Irish boy, as a Cockney with a Cockney
song. She had a Scotch fling, and came out as an American
sailor with hornpipe. For this number she was soon practiced with the snare-drum, and joined loudly in the
medley and walkaround. Her parts were increasingly in
blackface or in the minstrel tone; she danced amid the
rising rattle of bones; and she soon adopted the favored
instrument of minstrelsy and made it her own, the banjo.

A minstrel named Jake Wallace had taught Lotta to
strum the banjo in the mountains—

"Walk into de parlor and hear de banjo ring,
  And watch de darkey's fingers while he picks it on de
    string—"

Lotta drew from the banjo the deep bell-like thrumming
resonance which was the art of the plantation negro, with
the crowded and changing rhythm which belonged to his

songs. With the whole blackface company joining in, patting juba, she would play and lead the chorus—

"Ruberii, de cinnamon seed, seed de Billy hop jis' in time,
Juba dis, Juba dat, round de kettle of possum fat,
A-hoop-ahoy, a-hoop-ahoy, double step for juberii,
Sandy crab, de macreli, ham, and half a pint of Juba—"

finally tossing her instrument to another player and joining in the breakdown. She had dozens of banjo numbers with jigs, songs, and pantomime—

"Before I left we danc'd two reels,
(De holler ob her foot war back ob her heels!)
I played on de banjo till dey all began to sweat,
Knock'd on de jaw-bone and bust de clarinet."

She played and sang the favorite *Ole Bull and Old Dan Tucker*, well known in California and long relished there since Ole Bull had played in the city and in the interior—

"Ole Bull he made his elbow quiver,
He played a shake and den a shiver,
But when Dan Tucker touch his string
He'd make him shake like a locus' wing. . . .

"Loud de banjo talked away,
And beat Ole Bull from de Norway,
We'll take de shine from Paganini,
We're de boys from ole Virginny. . . ."

Lotta not only had a virtuosity on the banjo which could mock and chase the violin; she could produce the double pantomime and restless mounting of the race in song and on the strings.

She played on the same bill with the accomplished Billy Birch when he offered *The Gay Gambolier* and matched her banjo with his bones. Young Ned Harrigan turned up from nowhere and joined her in duets at Gilbert's and the Bella Union. She topped the bill at the What Cheer with young Johnny de Angelis, and played with some of her mountain minstrel companions at Rowena Granice's theater, the Union. The great "interrogator" of the mid-century, W. H. Bernard, was in the company at Maguire's, as was Charley Backus, one of the enduring San Francisco quartet. Ben Cotton was there, accomplished in aged darkey acts, quavering with new variations of the *Cum Plum Gum,* dancing the slow weaving rhythms of the *Essence of Old Virginny.*

These were all lusty players with an immense range, able to swing from a grotesque exuberance to a plaintive strain. The day was well over when women easily dominated the California stage; variety was a highly masculine theater, and attracted mainly an audience of men. Lotta might follow on the bill a crew of minstrels in character parts, booming out a highly favored parody of the Ghost Chorus from *Somnambula,* in which the whole company acted out the terror of the haunted night with pantomime

THOMAS MAGUIRE

LOTTA. THREE PORTRAITS FROM THE '60'S

and recitative in rich voices. She followed, quickly gaining the coveted later places on the bill; she was headlined
on the hangers. She danced with these accomplished
players, vied with them, took their pace and kept her own.

For all these minstrels the field constantly widened, as
under Maguire or less-known managers companies were
sent to the interior to meet the demand for variety there,
or to the new cluster of stormy fortune-making camps in
Washoe. Another great acceleration was afoot on the
Coast. A few straggling adventurers wandering into the
high waste region on top of the Sierras in search of gold
had come back with some lumps of blue mineral that
looked like lead, saying that the stuff was abundant in the
bleak valleys there. The lumps proved to be almost pure
silver; and a new hunt for fortune began. Not only silver
but gold in unbelievably lavish quantities was discovered
in Washoe; the long bare undulating mountains seemed
made of precious metal. Huddled groups of iron-roofed
houses sprang up almost overnight, and became Virginia
City, Gold Hill, Carson City. On the way to these heights
men were massacred at Truckee by warring Pi-Utes: but
these gory onslaughts hardly created a pause. Crowds of
prospectors toiled through the Yuba Gap, climbed through
one or another pass by pack-train, crept into the new
chosen land by whatever trail they could find.

In the wild and crowded towns the same demands for
the offset of entertainment arose which had brought actors

hurrying to the Coast in the days of '49. In Virginia City a theater was opened only a few months after the town was founded. Maguire promptly sent a company, and soon built a theater of his own, which was opened by Julia Dean in the midst of wind that rained gravel on the roof and against the windows and all but tore the roof from the theater.

Up to Washoe by stage went many companies, playing at the California camps along the way. Stage-coaches were often overturned by the Washoe Zephyr. Houses were overset like stacks of cards. A mule was blown high over Virginia City from Mount Davidson to Sugar Loaf Mountain. With the breaking of the rains avalanches of stone, timber, sand, would roll down the mountain-sides, bearing destruction. The struggle for gold or silver was hardly less desperate than the struggle for life, as men fought through the streets, as they strove for dips, spurs, and angles, as tunneling tore through the mountains. An immense speculation began—gambling on the greatest scale the country had known. In the Silver Land, so melodiously named, so wildly inhabited, the rewards were immense for players who could capture the attention of that closely throttled population. Lotta played there more than once. Cool as ever, Mrs. Crabtree arranged these trips; after all, her first schooling had been in the midst of scenes not essentially different. But records of those gusty communities have gone into oblivion like the splintered relics of their habitations: only a slight picture remains of Lotta dancing there in the melodeons or at Maguire's, a small figure in that gray tempest.

In 1862 the Crabtrees set out on a long circuit which included not only the sagebrush towns of Washoe but an ample round of California mining camps. Hard travel was ahead, for they started out in mid-winter; but the company had its own coach and outrider, and they were a convivial crew, accustomed to play together. Jake Wallace was manager, a tall, genial, lazy comedian, quick of wit and accomplished with the banjo, but willing to let Lotta outstrip him. Tom LaFont, a comedian who could make a trombone both stirring and funny, was one of the number; the Crabtrees had played with him before in the mountains. A young woman, mentioned as a balladist, was a member of the company. An actor named Keene stretched the accordion, another played the violin; and Mrs. Crabtree, making every edge cut in the way of returns, again played the triangle, and occasionally did an impersonation or even sang. The outrider with his drum wore a cut-glass pin so large and whitely glittering that the newspapers in the larger towns along the way charged double for hangers and advertising, but the company prized the pin, and decided the effect was worth the cost.

Through a wet February they worked through the southern mines and back again; but the rains had remained heavy, and as they went north from Sacramento toward Auburn the mud grew so deep that the horses were hardly able to drag the coach up the hills. The American River was in flood, with the approach to a main bridge washed away, leaving a chasm of mud and swirling water. As the coach plunged into the water and sped across, timbers cracked, and the whole bridge went down into the raging water as the coach dipped again into the torrent on the further side. In a rising storm the company traveled back through the slough of the valley to Sacramento, and played for a time at a melodeon with Biscaccianti. Houses were only fair; the troupe set out once more for the middle mining towns. At Iowa Hill they encountered ardent Union sentiment, and gave a grand patriotic program with Wallace singing *The Anthem of the Free*, and Lotta in a Topsy act which drew a hailstorm of money on the stage and applause in the house. But as they again traveled northward and at last reached southern Oregon, the atmosphere for patriotic numbers became less genial. In one village they were greeted by a rebel yell as soon as the curtain went up: the audience hissed when the opening Union airs were sung. Wallace advised Lotta to change her number—a sailor act with drum and flag and horn-pipe—for fear the company might be mobbed. Lotta's knowledge of the issue rested largely on her minstrel acts; but she was pledged to the Union side; she had grown increasingly fond of taking boys' parts; and her

temper was gusty in the face of opposition. "She said she
would give it if they hanged her that night," said Wallace. "She faced a cold and relentless audience and they
never gave her a hand." She won the tribute of a neutral
response; but the troupe moved rapidly out of the village as soon as the performance was over.

They pressed on over rough roads to Portland, and returned by steamer to San Francisco, where Lotta at once
began an increased number of engagements. Her round
of houses now included the Willows near the Mission: "a
sylvan retreat," as it was called on the bills, that had the
air of a foreign pleasure ground, with its park-like enclosure and flowing creek where black swans dipped. The
Willows boasted a menagerie, with a panther, a tiger, a
crocodile, a boa-constrictor, and a large number of strange
birds. Balloon ascensions were held there, and tight-rope
performances. Little tables were set outside, and a merry-
go-round played in the distance where ladies in hoop-
skirts and high little feathered hats trounced adventur-
ously around in a slow whirl. There were no back rooms
at the Willows; an air of domesticity, lacking in the
melodeons, pervaded the place, which was largely patronized by the French colony.

Miss Lotta, who had now reached the age of sixteen,
also wore hoop-skirts showing her slim ankles, of which
she had grown vain, and stiff little round hats hardly
larger than Mexican dollars, turned up behind with a

miniature feathery brush. She sometimes appeared in the costume as she sang pensive songs like *Willie, We Have Missed You* or *Dear Mother, I'll Come Home Again* or *The Soldier's Funeral*. But her changes to blackface

were rapid; and she now appeared almost invariably in the
concluding farce. A brief comedy called *The Soldier's
Bride* was "arranged expressly for Miss Lotta." She came
out in *Melodramatic Sally* and a burletta entitled *The
Swiss Cottage*, and in a farce which had long been popular,
if offered with fresh diversions, *Jenny Lind*. Lotta took
the part of Jenny Leatherlungs with mock shakes, trills,
and bravura, a few oddly interpolated minstrel songs, and
as much comic by-play as she chose to introduce. She
played at an increasing number of firemen's benefits,
which were always an index of public esteem; she gave acts
at the old American Theatre and at the new Metropolitan.
If she needed a final fillip of assurance this quickly came
in the relentless rivalry of the Worrell Sisters, three
vivacious and talented young actresses to her one, who
sometimes appeared a multitude.

The Worrells had been on and off the California stage
for several years; their father had been manager of a
circus and still had a hand in theatrical affairs. If they
never had the delicacy of appearance and light theatrical
touch which gave Lotta's acts distinction even at their
rowdiest, or her quaint charm of appearance (the Worrells tended to be swarthy and stout) they were amply
resourceful, with a gift for comedy and a histrionic talent
which was later to come into considerable recognition.
They fought Lotta with all the means at their command.

This warfare was staged mainly at Gilbert's, a popular

little theater with an absurd high balcony upstairs in front with flags flying, which looked like a booth at a fair. In so tiny a place there was only one dressing-room for actresses, a minute low-ceiled box within the flimsy box of the theater, with the usual rough shelf for make-up running around three sides, the usual mirror hung askew, a few hooks, and a handful of costumes bursting out of a champagne basket. From this crowded, microscopic battle-field Lotta emerged for her highly competitive acts. Some-times she topped the hangers, sometimes one or all of the Worrells did.

But the Worrells had their following; they mixed with people of the theater; Lotta, with all the friendship which she seemed easily to win from fellow-actors, suffered from the disadvantage of isolation. Except when they were in the mountains the Crabtrees seldom mingled with the shifting mob of actors; they hardly seemed theater people at all. The line "Miss Lotta the Unapproachable" un-wittingly summed up the case. That ring of fire which her mother had first drawn around the child was now widened and burned more fiercely. Even outside the thea-ter Lotta had few companions. In her old age she remem-bered that in these years a likely lad who owned a horse had wanted to take her driving. Mrs. Crabtree had turned him away; and afterwards Lotta, pensive and friendly, had contrived to sweep the front porch in the hope of at least another glimpse of this possible companion.

In the theater she lacked anything but the most casual association with other actors. Players everywhere, even the solitary Forrest, found the old greenroom something of a school. If variety houses had small space for formal assemblages, at Maguire's or the other larger theaters Lotta failed to join even in the usual lively offstage encounters. All theaters still had bars; the other acts were often sufficiently saucy. Mrs. Crabtree or some trusted vice-regent whisked Lotta in and out of the variety houses as vigilantly and swiftly as in an earlier day during their first ventures at the gambling saloons.

The odd circumstance was that Lotta seemed to possess an unflagging momentum of her own. Her routine was hard; she often had performances on the same night at both Gilbert's and the Willows. She still was deeply depressed before she went on to the stage: but once there she became a small skyrocket of fresh life and mirth. It was as if all the suppressed energy, all the unused capacity for other contacts, all the diverse pleasures which under other conditions she might have had, were poured out on a small wooden semi-circle with its painted flats before a darkened house. Her temper and her native force, which elsewhere had a slight outlet, here came into full play. She dashed into theatrical strife as if she liked it. Her small fists—unusually small—were often clenched like a prize-fighter's; she had a willful child's rage and determination in the face of disparagement; and competition in the mountains had given her both zest and training for a hearty matching of parts. Her black eyes flashed and danced as she fought the Worrells on their own ground. It was in the final walkaround that competition with her triple rivals became most acute. This massed assemblage grew into a fierce affair, as the trio and the single player strove to surpass their own established effects by novel turns. The Worrells all but crowded Lotta off the stage at times by their picturesque insistence, mocked her, toiled to outstrip her pace or to draw their own impersonations with more vigorous strokes. In that garish and hardy struggle Lotta continued to flourish, sturdily mocking in return, and as an actress acquiring a more roistering touch, an emphatic projection of character which were later ascribed to the Bowery but which actually sprang from the variety halls of San Francisco.

For this heightened mode she found plenty of encouragement in places where as a child she had caught her first high-colored view of theatricals, in the streets of San Francisco. Scant as was her personal experience, she could not have missed the pattern: no one could. San Francisco was still a milling, moving, outdoor city in spite of unpropitious weather, lit by gaslamps as the fog rolled in, by streaming light from places of amusement, or the glaring torches of small vendors and card-tricksters. The six city blocks bounded by Sacramento, Kearny, Jackson, and Sansome—thus including the edge of Portsmouth Square—contained many of the old buildings of earlier mining days, with wrought-iron balconies, odd doorways, intimate small glittering windows, and many a convivial retreat. Luscious odors floated out. Terrapin had been a mouth-watering legend in this quarter since the earliest years, when drinks like Moral Suasion, Silver Spout, and Vox Populi were in vogue. Fanciful names still persisted, with fanciful dishes. Broiled quail, fine game, delicate punches, a succulent French cooking, were staples here. This region, now verging more toward the south than the similar haunt of the early fifties, was the habitat of miners down for a holiday, artists, actors, journalists, all the careless expressive fraternity.

Along Montgomery and Kearny streets of a late afternoon might be seen an extended promenade, if not always of fashion, at least of character or caricature. Here on a large scale was a native walkaround, relished by every one who watched or took part. In a sense the whole parade was composed of actors. A sprinkling of shabby players might stroll past with an unusual display of fawn capes, high hats, and thin sticks: but they were only one element in a histrionic scene. Every character was boldly or fanci-fully delineated. A writer could be told by sheaves of papers sticking from his pockets at conspicuous angles. Miners still swaggered in their old high-booted masquerade. Chinese women minced by in gorgeous costume, part of the Orientalism that wound like a rich ribbon around the city.

Here too drifted a group of strange personages who could never have flourished except in a city of lavish humor with a *flair* for character and drama. They had grown into the life of San Francisco for a period of years, some of them from its beginnings, provided for out of generous pockets when they lacked food or a roof, sometimes jeered at by rascally gamins, but in the main encouraged and even solemnly courted. The Great Unknown was the only one of the company who did not receive alms. Tall, finely proportioned, with a graceful bearing and good features, black curly hair, imperial, and mustache, he seemed to have no occupation except the afternoon promenade. Unless he had traveled in disguise he had arrived on no steamer; nor had he been observed in the mountains. He had no friends and no bank account, though he was always in funds. Once a party of sporting men tried to break his reserve by bumping into him roughly on the street; without a tremor of expression he showed himself a polished boxer. In later years he was missed; at length his rooms were opened, and were found to be exquisitely neat, obviously arranged for departure. Not a scrap of evidence as to his identity was found there, nor was he seen again.

When the character known as George Washington

stepped off the steamer with an early crowd of argonauts some one had remarked the stately resemblance. He had dropped his pick and found a resplendent costume. Though it was freely suspected that he had only discovered an easy means of gold-hunting, his mimic and implacable calm forbade further inquiry. He supplemented his appearance by occult labor, telling fortunes in a secluded corner of Martin and Horton's saloon, and during the wild days on the Comstock gaining not a little reverent acclaim by successful predictions of the market. If he was offered less than four bits for his prophecies he stonily declined to take the money. Given more, his *hauteur* became intense. He never earned his keep: but he appeared appropriately well nourished; and his tricorn hat, frilled shirt, and handsome uniform were regularly renewed.

The Fat Boy was Bouncer at Maguire's, and paraded his occupation by an authoritative roll along the streets. The shabby little Guttersnipe and the equally shabby but florally decorated Rosie hovered on the outskirts of the procession, and maintained their almost too frankly stated make-up of poverty, however ample the *largesse* bestowed upon them. Prime favorites and prime actors were the two dogs, Bummer and Lazarus, so highly cherished in the region through which they roamed that a whole contradictory epic arose as to their origins and career: but there was no doubt that Bummer first received crumbs from Lazarus' ample supper, or that each found and carried food to the other in times of misfortune, or that each had a neat and waggish aptitude for assuming the part indicated by his name. An actor once said that they were superlatively good actors. Occasionally they appeared on the variety stage, with sly clownishness, and were ardently applauded.

Except for this pair each member of the group walked alone, or at least was oblivious of the others. The most solitary was the most pretentious in his claims, the Emperor Norton, Emperor of California, sometimes of the United States, always the Protector of Mexico. A Scotch Jew who had come to San Francisco in '49, Joshua Norton had accumulated a fortune by merchandising, and was ruined when a corner which he had secured had been broken by an unexpected shipload of provisions. He retreated into shadow for four years, and came forth with regal claims. He too assumed a uniform, with epaulettes and pinchbeck decorations, a soldier's cap, or on gala days a high silk hat with a cluster of chicken or turkey feathers in front. But whatever the disguises of the pseudo-Washington, there could be no doubt that Norton was mad; his strange impelling glance into space imposed itself even upon a mediocre artist who painted his portrait. With dreams of empire he ordered the building of a bridge which was to span the bay, and issued mandates to judges in every court as to defendants whom he favored.

Space was always found for his proclamations with their red paper seals; his script was honored, and seldom written for large sums. If he ventured into places of dignity Norton I was never tedious, never outstayed his welcome, and could match an occasion by his bearing. Dressed more magnificently than usual he once slipped into a chair on a platform at an assemblage intended to honor Dom Pedro de Braganza, the last Emperor of Brazil. No one laughed, though the whole room was tense with momentary mirth.

No one laughed when he entered a theater; occasionally a whole audience would arise, as by a sudden tolerance for human vagaries. Norton I would draw up his stubby figure to its full height, and bow. He always saluted actors on the street, was a favorite with them, and was uncommonly intelligent in his brief, clipped conversation on subjects other than that of his own position, or the sad case of Napoleon III, at whose death he had put on mourning.

In San Francisco of the sixties, as fortunes were wildly made or lost on the ledge through sudden rich strikes, as speculation rose with fury in the city, gaining a thousand times upon the gambling instinct which had always thriven there, as men still tided up and down the rivers and mountains, and treasure went out in solid millions by steamer, there was still ample room for these odd, outlandish figures. In those heated roaring years, far noisier than the era of the first gold rush, minor tolerances and perceptions might have been lost: but they were not. In the youthful, even uncouth and undeveloped city a life remained which seemed rooted in something like a generous whole of human understanding or endeavor, not a single part. Idiosyncrasy had a place. There was room for the play of character. Tolerance was an active element as in the earlier days, and unconsidered pleasure. Here were memory and legend, already more ardently possessed and more passionately fought over than in most regions of longer history.

Appropriately, another figure in the early free and striking scale appeared in San Francisco in these years. This was Adah Menken, who arrived in midsummer 1863, and obliterated every other theatrical interest. Maguire had brought her to play *Mazeppa,* for a fabulous sum. Like Lola Montez she came enveloped in legend; and strangely enough some lasting impress of that earlier adventurer seems to have been stamped upon Menken's mind—was it an emulation, or an obscure purpose of rivalry? Almost surely she had known Lola in New Orleans and New York, not only on the stage but in literary circles which each had joined. Both were said to resemble Lord Byron and cultivated the resemblance. In one of her lawless moods Menken remarked of Lola, "She began with a king and ran down the scale through a newspaper man to a miner. I began with a prize-fighter, and I will end with a prince!" The prize-fighter was Heenan, the Benicia Boy, well known in San Francisco. But Menken had not begun with Heenan, as she said: an earlier marriage seems to have preceded even her brief alliance with the Jew, Alexander Menken, through whom she was converted to the Jewish faith.

Most of her adventures had become the subject of fable. "No," she said scornfully to one of her new friends in San Francisco of her reported marriages, "I never lived with Houston; it was General Jackson, and Methusaleh, and other big men." But out of the welter of stories a consistent purpose appears. Lola Montez was an opportunist, seizing whatever vehicle came to hand, hoping to turn it into a chariot of triumph. Menken reached blindly toward some form of artistic expression. She had translated Homer at the age of twelve, had danced for a year in the ballet at the French Opera House in New Orleans, had gone to Havana and the City of Mexico with the Montplaisirs. On her return she had buried herself mysteriously in Texas, where she was said to have been captured by Indians and rescued by Texas rangers, and perhaps learned her fine horsemanship. Again in New Orleans she wrote her little volume called *Indigena,* and appeared there in a production of *Fazio.* At a tangent she had studied sculpture, and learned much of the technique which she employed on the stage. She had at last gone to New York with the determination to write. But though she promptly enough had become a member of the group at Pfaff's, and knew Whitman, though she gained the interest of many persons of taste who were inclined to give her assistance, she failed to find a secure place as a writer, and was forced to return to the stage, as a dancer, a pantomimist, and actress. She was soon playing her famous rôle in *Mazeppa*.

With an obstinate fling she also played *Lola Montez;* with a touch of brutal humor she even played the burlesque immediately after Lola's death. But it was in *Mazeppa* that she made a lasting impression throughout the country and on the Coast. That abortive circus performance, descended from the poetry of Byron, had been a favorite play on the American stage for more than thirty years in rude forms. By Menken it was given a new and daring level. Many persons believed that she had broken down the last barriers of decency; then and afterwards derogatory critics declared that it was Menken who inaugurated the nude drama. Perhaps she did: but she indubitably transformed a tawdry equestrian play into something which meant a reversion to poetry.

Every sensitive observer felt the beauty of her simple poses. "All grace—a model for the sculptor and painter!" cried one of these, remarking her changing attitudes in the clash with broadswords in *Mazeppa*. As her momentary postures appear in little *carte de visite* photographs, turned now the warm gray of marble which has long been buried in earth, the purity of outline seems that of the earlier Greek sculpture. She wore the Greek chiton; the perfection of her physical beauty then and in the moment when she all but stripped for the perilous ride must have smote the contemporary vision with greater force because of the ruffled, high-waisted disguises with which the feminine figure of the time was masked. But she possessed something more than a gift for fine attitudes; for many in her audiences her voice transcended every other impression. In the opening scene of *Mazeppa*, as she paused for a moment, then called a summons, the simple syllables took on an unaccustomed vibrancy. She kept a poised but rapid action throughout the play, which reached a climax in the ride up the steep wooden crags that all but pierced the netted sky-curtains.

The runway was narrow; she was strapped to the wild horse of Tartary—a great sorrel; a slip meant almost certain death. Once on the lower reaches of the ascent, at Albany, her horse had slipped; she had saved herself by skillful horsemanship. Her performances of *Mazeppa* always verged toward such episodes; the climactic effect was sheer melodrama. But she was playing now in a country where horsemanship was a second language, subtly understood, and melodrama part of life. The effect of her command as she climbed higher and higher for the final salute became something far more than an exploit, and reached a high point in the art of the theater.

If Menken had been content to give only *Mazeppa* she

might have become something of a classic; but as a practical affair she was obliged to have relief from the strain of the performance. Her restless, ungrounded temperament might have overflowed into cruder forms in any case. If her voice was declared to have the quality of a harp, she could use it when she chose like any of the instruments in a minstrel band. She played Corinthian Tom in *Tom and Jerry*, and the broad rôle of Polly Crisp in *An Unprotected Female*, singing a song which Lotta had made a favorite in the melodeons, *The Captain with his Whiskers Gave a Sly Wink at Me*, singing it with a gusto quite unlike Lotta's light and mischievous rendering. She gave French and Italian songs in both tenor and soprano voices. She seemed to be obsessed with protean changes. She offered impersonations of Charlotte Cushman, Edwin Forrest, Edwin Booth, and a dozen others, slipping these into her lighter plays as if these serious actors had assumed the frivolous rôles. She played five characters in *A Day in Paris*, three in *The French Spy*, a quartet in *Black-eyed Susan*. The majority of these were masculine parts. And if *Mazeppa*, even with her poetic touch, was sheer melodrama, her other plays constantly went over into a broad sensationalism. She played the long and difficult *Jack Sheppard*, which was still regarded as a wicked play. In *The Pirates of the Savannah* she had another ample melodrama, and reveled in it, appearing in the rich costume of

the fortunate *picaro*, showing another Menken, with a
curly boyish head and a youthful swagger.

For more than a month she played in San Francisco to
thronging audiences, then abruptly retired. She had been
welcomed by the small growing literary circle which included Bret Harte, Ina Coolbrith, Charles Stoddard, and
Adah Clare, who had been a member of the group at
Pfaff's, was known there as the Queen of Bohemia, and
was a friend of Menken's. Among this group Menken
created something of a *salon*, and found a clear and quiet
backwater. In the weeks that followed she wrote a bold
and sensitive critique on contemporary poetry in the
United States, *Swimming Against the Current*, which discussed the difficulties that had beset Poe and Whitman;
this was published in the *Golden Era*. She wrote and published in the same paper most of the poems which were
later to appear in her volume *Infelicia*, as well as others,
delicately lyrical, that have never been reprinted.

Her verse must be read as passionate autobiography
rather than as poetry—

> "Myself! alas for theme so poor,
> A theme but rich in fear . . ."

Her free rhythms have usually been ascribed to the influence of Whitman, but they seem rather to have sprung
from the writings of the Hebrew prophets. She kept the

Jewish Day of Atonement; her theater was closed then. She seems to have kept as well some sort of faith with Alexander Menken, whom she had married long before, though she apparently never saw him from the time of their separation, and was now after several other alliances married to the gentle satirist, Orpheus C. Kerr, who had accompanied her to San Francisco.

During these three or four months Menken became a familiar figure among the throngs on the streets. "Who of those days does not remember that graceful, yellow figure in the streets of San Francisco—in a single garment of yellow silk? I doubt if any other woman in the world could wear a dress like that in the winds of San Francisco and not look ridiculous," wrote Joaquin Miller. Yellow, the suggestion of light, seemed to have invaded her imagination. Miller saw her once in her hotel lying on a yellow skin with her head to the fire like an Indian, robed in a single piece of yellow silk. Once they rode together out the scoured road to the Seal Rocks; their horses plunged belly-deep in the sand beyond the Cliff House. Menken shouted with pleasure. "I was born in that yellow sand, sometime, and somewhere," she cried, "in the deserts of Africa, maybe." Miller said that she talked as he had never heard a woman talk before, of the color, the lion color, the old-gold color, the sun, the light, the life of the moving mountains of sand. "She seemed very happy, half wild." Then she suddenly threw herself into the sand, sobbing. She had gone back to the theater, either through Maguire's insistence, or because she had determined for herself that her poetry lacked an authentic power. "They are killing me at that old playhouse," she cried.

Difficulties had arisen at rehearsal, which may have grown out of her own mood. Junius Booth, now manager at Maguire's and in the company, sneered and prophesied failure. In the action with broadswords in *Mazeppa* either Menken or another actor nearly stabbed Booth, who roared with anger and left the theater, vowing never to return. He came back, but the confusion was unabated. At last, on Christmas Eve, after a brief season in Sacramento, the new engagement began, and proved full of storms. Menken took a dangerous fall in *Mazeppa*. She insisted on repeating the play, doubled in another equestrian drama, *Rookwood*, and seemed bent on startling her public. Having run through her usual repertoire, she produced a startling burletta called *The Three Fast Women, or Female Robinson Crusoes*, an English piece which was easily transformed into a local play with a realistic picture of Squarza's, many local characters and local hits, and a minstrel scene in which Menken played the bones end in blackface. In this piece she took nine characters, five of the men's parts, played them with an unbroken gay insolence, and then dashed off to Virginia City for an engagement at Maguire's New Opera House.

The iron-faced town was perpetually shaken, as every

mine was being worked with a great rumble of machinery and thousands of tons of quartz were crushed. Racing for high stakes, gambling, every form of theatricals flourished. Five legitimate companies and six or seven variety troupes were often playing at Virginia City at the same time, if not in the theaters, in any kind of contrived hall. Artemus Ward had recently given his monologues there, drawn to the Coast by Maguire's famous telegram asking him what he would take for forty nights. Ward's sojourn in Virginia City had been as convivial as his reply had promised. Early one winter morning he had tramped over the roofs of the town with chosen spirits from the *Territorial Enterprise*, Goodman, Dan de Quille, Dagget, and Mark Twain, as a closing episode. Not least of the diversions in the place were the hoaxes devised by that liberal crew in the columns of their paper, rough and gory like that which spelled war upon the San Francisco *Bulletin*, or simple, like the tale of the petrified man, which was devised to snare a coroner, and was copied in good faith by many exchanges.

This clan wrote the dramatic notices for their paper, usually in the form of an elaborate symposium. Before Menken arrived they had agreed to deride her: but when they saw her in *Mazeppa* their plans were overturned— or did they agree upon another elaborate hoax? At least their praises were so ardent as to excite the jealousy of the remainder of the company, some of whom inserted gags at Goodman's expense in the next evening's performance. Menken stopped the play and called upon the manager to make a public apology to Goodman. This he declined to do. The next night she refused to take her part. A large audience had to be dismissed. At the following performance she relented; and Mark Twain's notice of her acting was copied by papers throughout the country. Apparently enchanted by her grace and her beautiful voice, the band on the *Enterprise* piled ecstasy on ecstasy in praising Menken during the remainder of her stay; they noted her "inaccessibility," and declared that she seemed "to hold the world in contempt."

They seemed to regard her as a distant goddess. Yet later in San Francisco Mark Twain indulged in a bald and exceedingly poor pun on her acting: and if Menken was inaccessible in mood it must have been during this single passage in her career. She had few reserves and an ingenuous convivial fashion of believing what she was told, if the manner were amiable. She might at certain moments have betrayed herself into joining in such a hoax. She departed at last, leaving the feud behind her which had begun with the first lavish eulogy in the *Enterprise*. If good players came to the theater they received no notice; poor ones were unmercifully scored, with such disastrous results that actors at last declined to play at Maguire's. The editors announced that they regretted this result, but declared out of loyalty to Adah Menken they could make no change in their policy until the manager at the theater was dismissed, and certain casualties—which included the suspension of the free list and theatrical advertising—were repaired. This solemn battle was prolonged for months, and the avowed henchmen of Menken won.

By one of those oblique acquaintances to which she seemed destined, Lotta knew Adah Menken during her entire stay in California, perhaps through the friendly Stoddard, who admired Lotta's dancing and was tolerated by Mrs. Crabtree in spite of her inclination to repel Bohemian acquaintances. Menken was fond of young people; and Mrs. Crabtree let the new association glide toward friendship, perhaps relishing unconventionalism when presented in a grand style, no doubt flattered by the attention of an actress who was creating a furor in the town. Quite conspicuously Menken had singled out the pretty little red-haired minstrel, went to see her dance at the variety houses, took her horseback riding to the Cliff House, where the pleasure of promenades along the balconies awaited them, with views of sea-lions and the bay, or the spectacle of carriage-racing along the curving highlands, or even horseback races for themselves along the hard beach. Racing had become an immense sport, with tracks near the city: both Menken and Lotta had a taste for it. Young Lotta was an expert horsewoman, even though she had attempted no such equestrian feats on the stage as Menken. At times they had driven through the

streets of San Francisco, an odd pair, Lotta in the plainer
elegances of the day, hoops and capes and bizarre little
hats, Menken in her free-flowing barbarous yellow.

How much of her new friend's career was known to
Lotta can only be guessed; even in her seclusion she must
have heard some of the more conspicuous episodes. But it
may be surmised that most of these slid away from her
attention; over a simpler temperament she was gaining
something of that impervious surface which belonged to
her mother. One can fancy her peering up with those wide
black eyes of hers—so black the pupils hardly showed—
wondering whether she would ever be like Menken. There
were to be differences indeed: for one, Menken was never
a comedian. Yet at her slight distance Lotta perhaps drew
certain conclusions from the career of her companion, because she liked her, perhaps because Menken capped ten-
dencies in the theater to which Lotta herself was attracted.
She too wanted to act in startling plays. Her mother still
envisioned Lotta as a star, not in the transitory glimmer-
ing of a minstrel bill, but in the legitimate theater; and
Menken, more than any other figure which had appeared
on the San Francisco stage for half a dozen years or more,
enclosed the dazzling possibility.

Lotta was now nearly seventeen: but the most extravagant notice she could draw from the critics spoke of her
as "a clever juvenile . . . the most talented juvenile
actress California has yet produced." Truly enough she

had gone steadily up in the theatrical scale; she was given many benefits; her performances were still popular. But the warfare with the Worrells had continued; the little minxes had bobbed up everywhere. The Crabtrees had become involved in a quarrel with a manager in one of the melodeons; for Miss Lotta nothing except variety seemed in prospect.

As by a concerted movement Lotta, Menken, and Junius Booth took their farewell benefits in the same weeks and left San Francisco. The decision to go to New York must have involved Mrs. Crabtree in more than one vexing question. She had no knowledge of the theatrical world there except what she had gained by hearsay. But perhaps her deepest problem was personal. Lotta had been singing and dancing for nearly ten years, almost without a break. The returns had been generous, often lavish; and Mrs. Crabtree was still a thrifty woman. She had contrived costumes out of remnants; it was not until she was twenty-one that Lotta had her first silk dress. They now had a comfortable accumulation of money, even a small fortune. Lotta possessed besides a quantity of golden plunder. By the time she was twelve she had been given fourteen gold watches, most of them lavishly tossed to the stage. Her heap of rich trinkets had steadily increased.

In later years both Lotta and her mother declared that they would never have turned to the stage if they had not been obliged to make a living. Yet they continued

now. Perhaps Lotta's talent created an irresistible momentum. No doubt Mrs. Crabtree had become the single-
minded manager. She had faded; she looked worn and
even delicate; she was not to keep the perennial freshness
which lasted Lotta through most of her years. But she
was to have sturdy renascences; and the outline of her
career and of Lotta's was settled, once and for all. The
two boys were left in San Francisco when Lotta and her
mother departed in the late spring of 1864, with Crabtree
in their train.

Once again they had moved opportunely. Menken,
playing her last engagements as in a whirlwind, had
seemed to draw change in her wake. There was something
momentous in the retirement of Junius Booth from the
California stage; it suggested a fundamental alteration
in the scene. He had been one of its earliest players, had
acted in nearly every important theater in San Francisco
and in the interior, had been actor-manager in many of
these, and in one way or another had been associated with
nearly every leading actor who had come to the Coast.
Through solid friendships he had woven himself into the
life of the city where he had lived so long.

Other changes followed. The Worrells soon left, likewise bound for New York. A few at a time the minstrels
began to filter away. Presently the San Francisco Minstrels, who in one or another combination had existed on
the Coast from the early period, left Maguire and went

to New York, where they gained an instant popular following which was to last for twenty years. New winds were blowing through the California theaters which seemed to strike Maguire with special force. His taste for musical grandeur set him on a transient road to ruin; at the moment his was hardly a friendly ambition. Some one said that there were two gigantic conflicts in the sixties: the Civil War and Maguire's battles with his opera troupes. Felicita Vestvali, the Magnificent, had him arrested for threats of personal violence, and then triumphantly sang at his theater in spite of his injunction. He expended a wrathful energy upon an obscure actor named McDougal, and was apostrophized by Mark Twain—

> "For shame! oh, fie!
> Maguire, why
> Will you thus skyugle?
> Why curse and swear
> And rip and tear
> The innocent McDougal?

> "Of bones bereft
> Almost, you've left
> Vestvali, gentle Jew gal;
> And now you've smashed
> And almost hashed
> The form of poor McDougal!"

When his theater was empty—which was often—Maguire stalked down to the front row, his face wreathed in smiles, his gambler's showy front more resplendent than ever. When the theater was full he looked under the darkest cloud, glared, stormed, threatened, was dissatisfied with every one from the diva to the call-boy. As if obscurely aware of coming events he attempted a few magnificent offerings in drama, and brought out the Keans and Edwin Forrest. But the Keans were a little remote; and Forrest, still smarting with bitterness after his long sword-play with Catherine Sinclair, was now actually ill, and played haltingly. His houses were empty; his engagement was curtailed; he had come for a hundred nights at Maguire's invitation, and played only thirty-five.

Then Maguire was harried by young Frank Bates at the Metropolitan, a high-spirited young manager who had acted at Mobile with his wife during the bombardment, and had perhaps gained there an arsenal of resource to add to talent. Frank Bates, fresh on the scene, fought Maguire at every point. He brought the Parepa-Rosas to San Francisco, the largest and most complete of the operatic troupes which had yet visited the Coast, made them a popular success, and thus administered a discipline which must have been galling to Maguire. And young Bates was firmly bent upon establishing a theater; he quickly drew about him the more accomplished of the actors who had remained in California, playing the legitimate drama. Other young players of talent began drifting in: Harry Edwards, John McCullough, Emelie Melville.

In the midst of these unsettling changes the tidings of Lotta's spectacular success in New York and Boston, Chicago and St. Louis, came in a flood. The theatrical sheets in San Francisco were full of notices about Lotta, now no longer Miss Lotta, never Lotta Crabtree, but simply and possessively Lotta. Even the San Francisco daily papers, which no longer gave the ample theatrical notices of earlier days, offered news of Lotta. She was a star. She had appeared at Niblo's, at Wallack's, at the Broadway, the Howard Athenaeum, the Boston Theatre, the Walnut Street in Philadelphia; she had traveled in the West and South; plays had been written for her; critics were trying to analyze her charm. Fulfilling her new ambition within a year or two, Lotta was now appearing on the legitimate stage, or its extravagant semblance. This was Lotta, whose playing as a variety actress Maguire had finally recognized, then overlooked.

The legitimate theater was in the ascendant in San Francisco, though Maguire missed the new drift. It may be fantastic to suppose that Adah Menken gave final impetus to a movement which had long had a vigorous subterranean life on the Coast. Ample esteem must be rendered that band of players who had maintained the legitimate stage in its less fortunate days, Mrs. Judah, Sophie Edwin, and the others. Not all of them were bril-

STREET CHARACTERS OF SAN FRANCISCO

Emperor Norton, George Washington, The Great Unknown, Bummer and Lazarus, and
Others. A Contemporary Cartoon by Edward Jump

ADAH MENKEN

liant actors; but they had developed a rich fund of knowledge of the theater; they were a nucleus for the great stock company which was presently to be formed. Variety too had sharply keyed up the formal theater, with its shattering gayety; many actors had moved back and forth from the legitimate to the variety stage. But the life of the theater in California had been nourished on spectacular character from the beginning; and in some sense the interest must remain an essential one for full theatrical expression. The power to throw character into a many-sided relationship, at the least the power by which rich temperament overflows its constraining vehicle: this remains the core of fine acting, the beginning if not the end. This Adah Menken had. Garish as were her plays, she entered the positive theatrical world where every element speaks with the others to unfold a concentrated dramatic meaning. If her ride up the wooden cliffs was a circus performance, it was also sheer theater, by the amplification of her voice, her gestures, her poses, the dynamics of character. She was often close to the variety stage in her bold impersonations: but she commanded the large focus of the complete play. Never a great actress, but with the scale and superabundant power that had always been manifest there, Adah Menken remained in the larger tradition of the California stage. Along with the flock of Mazeppas that spread over the country, she perhaps unleashed a larger freedom.

VI

EXTRAVAGANZA

CONFIDENT OF LOTTA'S TALENT, MRS. CRABTREE SEEMS to have thought that this had only to be displayed in New York and a new career would promptly begin. Soon after they landed in the early summer of 1864, she had engaged Niblo's Saloon, a small hall of entertainment which enjoyed only a reflection of the favor that came to Niblo's Garden; and in momentary weakness she put Crabtree forward as lessee and proprietor. Crabtree had a fine upstanding figure and a look of extraordinary self-respect. Mrs. Crabtree was still faintly proud of him: but it may be doubted whether he added wisdom or power to the undertaking. With Lotta billed as the California Favorite, joining with an obscure company, they offered a variety program, with dances, banjo solos, songs, and farces; among others Lotta gave as an afterpiece her expert burlesque of the old *Jenny Lind*. She received the tribute of considerable discussion in the New York *Clipper* and elsewhere: but this swung toward a discouraging conclusion. Lotta's versatility was praised, her skill with the banjo considered near the top rank. "She can dance a regular breakdown in true burnt cork style and gives an Irish jig

as well as we have ever seen it done. She has a pleasing
countenance, looks charming on the stage . . . and knows
exactly how to put an audience in good humor. She would
prove a valuable star to any music house in the country."
This was the rub. "Her style is certainly not intended for
a first-class audience, concert halls being her proper stamp-
ing-ground."

Lotta played for only a few nights in New York, crept
into a minor engagement in Philadelphia, and at last began touring the smaller towns of the Middle West with a
third-rate manager. Sometimes she offered variety bills,
as these were almost sure to command an audience: gradually Mrs. Crabtree increased the number of plays. Lotta
came out in *Nan the Good for Nothing*, which was to remain in her repertoire for years, and contained a kind of
part she was always to favor, that of the ragged little
romp who dips into all sorts of rough comedy business,
dances like a street arab, is pert and rude but engaging,
and comes to a good end.

Over the same circuit they went again and again,
through Pittsburgh, Cincinnati, Louisville, Buffalo, with
occasional flying visits to Philadelphia, or into the South
like carpet-baggers, seeking what they could find, joining here and there with battered stock companies. It was
an arduous experience. A few days of rehearsal with
strangers preceded the brief runs. All her life Lotta was
"a hard study." She pored with difficulty over her parts;

in the hours before a performance she was as reluctant as ever to appear. Upon her mother, as in earlier days in the mountains, fell the burden of keeping her in good spirits, making difficult arrangements, even of playing: many times Mrs. Crabtree took minor parts. She was far quicker than Lotta in learning lines, and could slip into almost any vacant place; she even occasionally took men's character parts. And from time to time, in the handsomer, less exacting rôles, Crabtree walked on, and was to do so for some years, as he continued to travel with his wife and daughter. Apparently his presence was required on these long tours for the conventions, as it had not been in the mountains of California. Wearing a topper and a long black cloak, he made a tall pretentious figure of a man, with his invincible air of leisure.

Lotta's stock of plays increased, and included moderately ambitious efforts like the boyish operetta, *The Pet of the Petticoats*, and the farcical *Captain Charlotte*. At McVicker's in Chicago an enthusiastic gentleman wrapped a handsome gold watch in sufficiently thick layers of handkerchiefs and hurled it to the stage as a tribute when she took the rôle of Tartarine in *The Seven Sisters*, sometimes called *The Seven Daughters of Satan*, a spectacle play of immense popularity, which included the characters of Pluto, Mrs. Pluto, a minstrel band, and a large number of showy scenes, among these the unexpected apparition of the Birth of Cupid in a Bower of Ferns. This delicate and somewhat irrelevant diversion provided a contrast with the full-flowered antics of Tartarine in blackface with minstrel songs, banjo numbers, breakdowns, jigs, hornpipes, reels, her lesser sisters joining in the chorus and final step-dances as in a walk-around. As Lotta played it, *The Seven Sisters* was nothing less than a female minstrel show verging upon melodrama by sudden shifts of startling scenery and action.

She swaggered and romped through all her parts with a lavish dispersal of songs, dances, banjo-playing, and even turns of the hand-organ. There was novelty in these offerings, novelty too in her youth and vivacity: advance engagements in which she headed the better local companies were soon assured her. A little more than a year after she had left San Francisco she wrote to a middle-aged friend there who had sometimes been permitted to take her to the variety halls for her performances and to bring her home again. Her letter was heady with triumphs. "Yes, we started out quite fresh, and so far things have been very prosperous. I am a continual success wherever I go. In some places I created quite a theatrical furor, as they call it, and so far our agent is such a gentleman and good business man that we are perfectly satisfied with him. He is also a man of money. His wife travels with him, and a more ladylike person we never had the good fortune to be in company with. . . . The Reens played one week and we returned to play one week after them.

I played to far the biggest houses but not so much money, for their prices were double. I have got up the far-famed play called *Fanchon* to play in Buffalo. The people were delighted and the theater not big enough to hold them. Now when I write to you and send you bills and notices, don't let any one see them, you can keep all the pleasure to yourself. When any one tells you that Smith is going to bring me back, you can tell him that you know better; we have not seen him and if we did we should not speak to him. We made up our minds when we left San Francisco we should never know a great number of people there any more, nor shall we. Why, Friend Billie, your heart would jump with joy to see the respect I am treated with here amongst the theater people. I'm a star, and that is sufficient, and making quite a name. But I treat all and every one with the greatest respect and that is not what every one does, and in consequence I get my reward. . . ."

"I'm a star . . . I'm a star!" The refrain sang through Lotta's letters. "I'm a star!" In her next letter to Friend Billie she had forgotten the animosities of the last months in San Francisco, and wanted to return, for friendship, and to display her new accomplishments.

"I yesterday received your kind letter, with bill and notices, which gave me much pleasure. But they made me feel quite homesick. . . . Well, suppose now we start for home in June and make a flying trip through the country for about six weeks and play new pieces, and open in good style at Maguire's. Do you think I would do well? If so, in your next letter let me know, for mother thinks I would do very well for six weeks—two weeks in San Francisco, two weeks in Washoe, and one week in Sacramento, and the last week in San Francisco before leaving for the States again to fulfill my fall engagements. Now be sure to tell me what you think of our plan. . . .

"While in Philadelphia we got a lady who has been very successful in her writings to write me a play. It is called *Mabbie Astray, or the Child of Trials*. We trust it may be a success. If so, I shall have the pleasure of playing it in San Francisco."

The time had not yet come when Lotta could race back to San Francisco for a driving six weeks at Maguire's or elsewhere, and skirt the country for another season's engagements. She had not reached New York again; and she lacked a striking new play of her own. No more was heard of *Mabbie*, which may have been dim in plot. But somewhere on a wide circuit, perhaps at Mobile or St. Louis, John Brougham saw Lotta and dubbed her "the dramatic cocktail," a title which Mrs. Crabtree tried in vain to suppress. The encounter was lucky. Brougham cast scenes from *The Old Curiosity Shop* into a play for Lotta; she was to double as Little Nell and the Marchioness. This was a triumph indeed, for Brougham was not only an accomplished actor, a successful and prolific playwright; he had been a pioneer since the late forties in an art toward which Lotta leaned, that of burlesque.

A positive turn of fortune had come at last: but Mrs. Crabtree, still the manager, warily stalked success. The new play, *Little Nell and the Marchioness,* was first produced at a small theater in Boston, the Continental, late in 1866; then once more Lotta went on tour, repeating it, only occasionally, through the West and South. Her new triumphs became a matter of record in the New York theatrical papers; during the spring of 1867 she was mentioned almost week by week. When in May she arrived in Jersey City a small tempest of questions arose. What would she do next? She retired with her mother to a farmhouse on Long Island for a rest. Later, with a casual air, as if theatrical productions were the least of their concerns, the Crabtrees established themselves at the Fifth Avenue Hotel. These patent maneuvers had their effect. Mrs. Crabtree was offered the great playhouse of the day, Wallack's. The time was midsummer, the weather so hot that nearly every newspaper column breathed it. Theatrical business was notoriously poor in New York at this season: but Wallack's was crowded for six weeks as Lotta played there. The *Clipper* declared that no other star or combination had achieved such a triumph.

With an apparently simple beginning Lotta took off in a familiar play, the romping *Pet of the Petticoats,* in which she sang Irish songs, danced Irish jigs, played the banjo,

and captured the good will of her audience. Then followed *Little Nell and the Marchioness*. A critic com-
plained that the dramatist had slighted the part of Little
Nell: but the entire play was something of an extravaganza, and became more liberal in its innovations the
longer Lotta played it. She did not relish the part of the
patient little seraph. Before going on she would knit her
brow and smooth it our again, would walk up and down
her dressing-room, saying aloud, "Now, I'm poor Little
Nell, and very, very serious. . . . I'm poor Little Nell
. . . *poor* Little Nell." This simple device seemed to
give her a sufficient assurance; she looked ethereal; the
audience was melted to sobs when in the final act the flats
were drawn off to discover old Trent kneeling in the
graveyard, and when, after this tableau had been fairly
apprehended, the back opened and Little Nell, celestial
in white fire, was seen ascending to Heaven.

But it was as the Marchioness, in the doubled part, that
Lotta came into her own. Ragged and dirty, in colloquy
with the Brasses, in the scene where she hungrily eyed the
mutton-bone, in her fantastic play-acting with Dick
Swiveller, or in the hardy encounters with Quilp, she sus-
tained a genuine character. The part was exaggerated, as
Dickens himself is often boldly overstressed: but Lotta
contrived a comic, wistful, passionate Sophronia who was
never actually sure that she was not a Marchioness, etch-
ing out the whole effect with secure and simple strokes

which she had learned long before in variety. Perhaps with this accomplishment she should have paused, but she did not. With a slighter grasp of character her humor might have obliterated everything else in the play; it became wild fun tiding past all bounds, from the slapstick of the mustard plaster that Sophronia hurled at Quilp to the by-play of breakdown and banjo in the scenes between the Marchioness and Swiveller. The plaster came full on; the prompt-book called for a pitcher of water behind the right center at this point; the minstrelsy matched any that the curious had beheld in any dedicated minstrel hall. Even the first encounter between the Marchioness and Swiveller broke into minstrelsy, with Lotta playing the banjo and Swiveller as end-man with the mutton-bone. The high point of this play was the fair, produced on a lavish scale, with tents and the Sybil's cave, Jarley's wax-works, the peep-show, part of the circus, the thimble-rig table, a throng of gypsies, a group fighting with broad-swords, a concourse of visitors drifting up and down, a parade of clown and pantaloon, and at last the Sable Minstrels with Sophronia dancing at their head in strange bright costume, singing song after comic minstrel song with jigs and reels and a final breakdown, and Quilp crying "There she is!" as he was hoisted up on the tight-rope by the acrobats.

Lotta's small dancing figure had a vitality which transcended even a high-colored massed effect on a large stage.

She possessed a personal quality which floated the entire extravagant production. It bordered on burlesque; she brought the play into a realm between reality and comic fancy: yet she kept intact the odd original pathos of her part. "Witchery" some of her critics called it, seeking to name her quality, "a freakish charm." Something that suggested delicacy was usually mentioned even when the critics declared that Lotta was not always entirely refined. A few fell back upon the observation that she was "a child of nature." It was plain that they were trying to name a highly original, contagious effect. With a wild freedom, a bold inflation which she had learned long ago in the mines, with a wealth and range of humor, the tiny creature had lifted the whole production into the realm of extravaganza, and at the same time impressed her own character upon her audience.

This gala season in New York had more than one hint of reminiscence: the Worrells were ascending theatrical heights at the same moment. They already had their own theater, the New York; and they soon had formed a friendly alliance with young Augustin Daly. In a year or two he dramatized Henry Ward Beecher's novel *Norwood* for their use and at their request; they also acted in his version of *Pickwick Papers*. If Lotta was to enjoy the sweets of triumph from the circumstance that their Dickens play soon perished while hers lasted for twenty-five years, at the moment she saw their first startling triumph in Daly's enduring melodrama, *Under the Gaslight*. To be sure there was no real part for one of the Worrells; she was obliged to walk on: but another of the sisters had the lead, the third a good character rôle; and the play was overflowing with novelty and terror. It was the first success in a type of play which was to overrun the boards for many years. Laura, the heroine, was thrown from a pier into the North River. Snorkey, the wounded guardian of Laura, was bound to a railroad track by the villain, and became the parent of a long line of worthy young men and women who were to endure that fate.

Copying Lotta, the Worrells introduced minstrel business into *Under the Gaslight*. But Lotta scattered minstrelsy with a lavish hand through all her plays. Within a few months she was back in New York at the Broadway playing Topsy, responding to half a dozen encores after her banjo numbers. She traveled again in the West and South, and played in *Little Nell and the Marchioness* to such packed, riotous audiences that Wallack and Davenport, in Chicago at the same time before empty houses, came out before the curtain and declared that they would not return until they had learned to play the banjo and dance a clog. In the autumn of 1868 Lotta was at the Boston Theatre, advertised by Junius Booth, its manager, as "Little Fairy Lotta," the "Diamond Edition of Dramatic Delights." Here she appeared in a melodrama of her own, *Firefly*, arranged from Ouida's *Under Two Flags*.

The play was considered daring. Lotta was a *vivandière*, a mascot, madcap, rebel, who wore her skirts six or eight inches from the ground, and smoked, freely and gracefully. She afterwards insisted that she learned to smoke from Lola Montez; certainly it must have been from that daring example or from Menken that she received the impulse to smoke on the stage: yet she seems to have kept an air which it was not their fortune to maintain, that of innocence, which carried her past the increasing rigor of the sixties. In *Firefly* she used dozens of reckless small pieces of business, with her incalculable air of distinction. Light and full of fire as the name suggested, she dashed through the rapid action of the play, leading the regiment, mixing with the soldiers, singing *Bright Champagne*, dancing on parapets with rollicking high steps which rivaled those of the famous Majiltons, and at last, as the action thickened, riding swiftly across the desert with a reprieve for her soldier lover, and—a little improbably—flinging herself in front of his body to receive the volley of bullets as she realizes that she is too late.

The hoyden in a dozen aspects became Lotta's substantial part. She rolled off sofas and showed far more than an ankle: pulling up her stocking she ran on to the stage in *Nan the Good for Nothing*: the movement, in an age when even allusions to stockings were considered depraved, became indescribably comic. She lifted herself to tables and swung her feet—another dashing innovation. Her short skirts were daring, as was her smoking: her repeated assumption of masculine parts was new. Hitherto these had been attempted only by actresses who were daring both on and off the stage, like Menken or Lola Montez. One of the Worrells had timidly begged to be excused from taking a guttersnipe's part, a small one, because she would be obliged to wear boy's clothes. Lotta would have reveled in it, if the part had been a lead; she already had half a dozen such major rôles.

In *The Little Detective*, another new play, she impersonated six characters, and as one of them, Harry Racket, came out in a fawn-colored sporting costume like one which Menken had affected, struck the same poses, smoked in the same casual fashion: the difference was that Lotta, the innocent Lotta, looked far more rakish. In speech and appearance her Barney O'Brien in the same play was in another world from Harry Racket. It was not only that her repertoire of Irish jigs and reels made a diversion; apart from these she developed a composite character which she might have been studying since the days when she came out on the little stage at Rabbit Creek. She was obstinate, highly boyish, with a strain of bold looks and inflexibility. Even at a close view she was unlike herself in any other part. As Mrs. Gamadge, the old nurse, make-up had some effect in her astonishing elderly appearance: but her elongated face, her quavering gestures, her questing talk with a touch of Cockney: these elucidated a character.

In the ordinary touch-and-go of the stage doubling is a gimcrack affair, obtaining its effects by crude surprise. Lotta was pleased with the sheer masquerade: it was a game for quick wits and a nimble body. But she boldly struck off comic character as well, even as she inflated her transformations. Likewise her saucy hoyden's parts, her daring pantomime, her smoking and short skirts became something more than novelty. She was shattering traditions as if she could not contain herself within stereotyped forms. She was already a comedian, or *comédienne*, as the stage prefers it, foot-loose, turning to new amusement whatever she touched, creating the airy structure of extravaganza in unlikely places.

Broad comedy for women was still rebellion. In a period when a delicate distance was considered an ultimate feminine quality, it was rebellion indeed to forget the prerogative of a languishing charm; it was nothing short of revolt to diminish the aura by which woman—it was hoped—might always be surrounded, and actually to laugh with an audience, thus shattering distance altogether. Few actresses even in the liberal California days had attempted it, even though a tradition for comedy had prevailed there.

Quickly and heedlessly Lotta broke a dozen traditions, as if she could not help it; she had scarcely a touch of the older stereotyped comedy; she seemed to improvise and often did. Yet she somehow escaped the usual penalties of innovation. She was not too novel for her time. Something in the rough and shattered mood that prevailed after the War responded to both her lawlessness and her gayety. Riding a high wave of popularity she dashed back to New York and Boston for engagements every few months, had extended seasons in Philadelphia at the Arch Street Theatre under the management of Mrs. John Drew, where she created a minor sensation by stopping the orchestra when the musicians failed in a lingering ragged rhythm for her soft-shoe dancing, and leading them herself until they found the true measure. Polkas were now dedicated to Miss Lotta, marches, nocturnes, mazurkas, waltzes and innumerable songs. The story became famous of her exclamation when a cat walked on the stage as she was coaxing her banjo. "Why, look at that great big cat!" she said, as if to herself, then gave a little shake and took up her part. Once on the stage she seemed to have no sense of herself as an actress or the audience as spectators. In Buffalo, singing a duet in an operetta, *Le Postillion,* she was encored seven times; pink and breathless, all but staggering, she laughed with pleasure and audibly asked her partner, "What do you say, Ben, shall we sing it again?" Yet natural as she was,

LOTTA. TWO PORTRAITS FROM THE '70's AND (*right*) AS THE MARCHIONESS

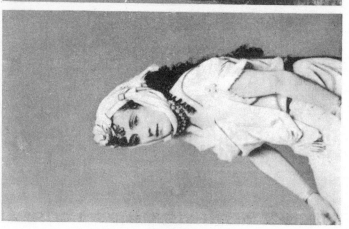

ADAH MENKEN

something trim and aloof continued to distinguish her acting; she already had begun to build up and widen her parts. The effect, with her humor and the daring of her plays, made impact after impact; in the effort to name her unaccountable quality her admirers turned to her origins: this odd spirited little creature had come out of the West. Seizing a garish phrasing, as Junius Booth had done, they called her the California Diamond.

Lotta went back to California for a brief season, in August, 1869, appearing with her usual timeliness at a turn of affairs. The empire of the far West, so long iso-lated, was now at last linked by steel rails with the East. National expansion had begun to throb there. The flam-boyant, rococo spirit flourishing abundantly in the East after the Civil War had its large counterpart on the Pacific Coast, in new ambitions and a new scale. Many changes were afoot: the old pioneer days were over. With the coming of the railroad, with the expanded develop-ment of the Washoe mines, the great boom in speculation, the widening of agriculture, a marked change had come over the face of the new country. Yet was it all change? Only perhaps a huger emphasis? Tiding up with fresh volume, the old life of the early fifties seemed repeated with increased noise and confidence. If gambling in gold slugs had been the obsession of booted miners down for a few days in San Francisco, now wild gambling in stock made a basic fabric. These were the days of the big bonanza, the frantic shuttling up and down of "feet" on the Comstock, of increasing fabulous fortunes and equal precipitous losses. If in the fifties men had rushed off to shovel gold sand on the northern shore, within a few years astute bankers were to be drawn by a fantasy which described the fields of Montana as sown so thickly with jewels that the dazzle of light was almost unbearable when the sun shone. Their own experts were sent to view the sight, and came back announcing that diamonds could be picked out of seams in rocks with the fingers, rubies and emeralds and sapphires scooped up by the hatful. If this hoax went the way of many another, with sharper losses, the brilliant imagery remained with an opulent strain of fancy.

Again in the midst of unbridled extravagance theatricals flourished. Another epoch had begun. That slow movement which had so disturbed Maguire took its predestined shape. A powerful and expert stock company had found a permanent stage in the new California Theatre, a spacious playhouse built by William C. Ralston, a gambler in old modes and new ones, with a vision of empire and a strong bias toward the theater. Excellently designed, with fine exterior arches and a wide lobby which ran around the three sides of the building, the California Theatre seemed designed both for the cultivation of actors and the pleasures of an audience. Few greenrooms had such dignity, few theaters such comfortable dressing-

rooms; sounds behind the stage were deadened. For the
audience ease reached the point of fantastic luxury. The
first three rows of the dress circle had legless chairs with
high backs, fixed with hinges and springs like rocking-
chairs. Family boxes at each side of the house seated a
dozen people; smaller ones were set irregularly in the
walls like martlet nests in the rocks, as an English visitor
remarked. Pit and dress circle merged together; galleries
rose, tier on splendid tier. If some of its effects were
sprawling and bizarre, none the less they provided excellent vision; and the whole large theater had an air of
extraordinary intimacy.

Night after night a familiar audience packed the theater, no longer in the casual costumes of the earlier days;
carriages rolled up; there was now a rich display, jewels,
gorgeous dresses, an air of worldliness; but it was the
schooled audience of the first years. The opening play
was *Money*, itself a reminiscence; given repeatedly in San
Francisco during the fifties, it was now produced with
a splendor that was a commentary on the times. Even
the occasion marked an epoch: the new theater was opened
in January, 1869, almost twenty years to a day after the
first tide of gold-seekers had emptied on the Coast. The
salutation, written by Bret Harte, was a conscious gesture
of both farewell and hail. The curtain, too crowded with
detail for beauty, was covered with Spanish scenes and
vignettes of early mining days. Like *Money*, many of

the plays presented were familiar. Shakespeare was revived in a series of magnificent productions, with a rota-
tion of actors in the leading parts. Even the gallery gods
knew many of the plays almost by heart. Here were both
knowledge of the theater and that leisure of mind which
could take pleasure in new interpretations.

The audience knew the older plays, and knew the
players. Some of that early group which had remained on
the Coast, weathering the winds of variety, were there,
with new actors who had continued the tradition of the
first theatricals, traveling during the middle sixties in
Washoe and the California mining camps. The most
talented had coalesced under the leadership of John
McCullough and young Lawrence Barrett. "Sometimes
we played stars, sometimes productions," said one of the
company. Visiting stars were part of the order at the California: John Brougham came, Adelaide Neilson, Sothern,
Edwin Booth, Modjeska. But the glory and promise of
the California Theatre was its stock company; it was un-
rivaled in its time; indeed, many actors have declared that
it has never been rivaled. Possessing an immense famili-
arity with the theater, its members slipped into any part.
Perhaps they seldom played with that complete subordi-
nation to the whole. Mrs. Judah can hardly be pictured
submerging herself even in a minor rôle. She never did;
few of these actors did. Almost all of them had been stars;
some of them had been managers; they had had a free

rein in breaking traditions; they had gone to school in theaters where large figures had fought their way and dominated as they could. Now they continued in the same mode. Their versions were lusty, full-bodied, sometimes overstressed, yet abundantly crowded with life. If they rarely subordinated themselves to each other, they gave themselves to the play, and the audience harvested a fresh and ample theater. Mrs. Judah's fine portrayal of the Nurse in *Romeo and Juliet* with Adelaide Neilson passed into something more than local tradition.

Lotta appeared at the California Theatre during its first unbroken season of three hundred nights. It was a formidable ordeal; she was playing before the most homogeneous and expert audience she had known, joining with a highly experienced cast. But her rise had touched popular imagination; her audience was friendly; at the opening performance of *Little Nell and the Marchioness,* every seat, every niche in the large theater was filled. After each climactic moment it seemed that the applause would never end. Smiling, enchanted, she was lavish with encores; on succeeding nights she reeled off her plays in rapid profusion. "See what I can do!" she seemed to cry; and she offered astonishment enough. Within the brief period since she had left California she had acquired what a theater-going public demanded, what seasoned players possessed, a repertoire. Not all of this was new; she offered her favorite *Nan the Good for Nothing,* the operatic

Pet of the Petticoats, the farcical *Governor's Wife*, with its reminiscent travesty of Lola Montez, the old but still popular *Family Jars*, *The Irish Diamond*, and *Captain Charlotte*. In many of these plays she doubled, thus presenting a dazzling display of characters. She brought out new afterpieces, and played Sam Willoughby in *The Ticket of Leave Man*, as well as her highly diverse rôles in *Little Nell*, *Firefly*, and *The Little Detective*.

The stage was large, her plays ambitiously mounted. The production of *Firefly* took on magnificence, with marching troops, a lavish representation of camps, the boom of cannon and cracking small firearms, and a panorama representing the ride over the desert. Lotta was surrounded by the new company: Barrett, McCullough, Harry Edwards, Raymond, and pretty young Emelie Melville were constantly in her support. Mrs. Judah played Mrs. Jarley. But even by that overpowering presence Lotta was unperturbed. Against those skillful positive personalities, on the large and showy stage, her small figure kept its concentrated life: from the moment she slipped into view she commanded the scene, and mixed reminiscence with surprise. As Andy Blake in *The Irish Diamond* and as Barney O'Brien in *The Little Detective* she harked far back to her first small adventure. All her parts were crammed to the brim with minstrel or melodeon business. But she dashed far beyond the knowledge or expectation of her audience. Some of her comedy was

considered "high-flavored and gamey." Where had she
caught it? From other minstrels? In her early days at the
Bella Union when she had been swiftly borne in and out?
She romped "with a reckless abandon of the laws of taste,"
observed one of the critics, who continued to praise her.
Her personal quality, vigorous yet delicate, overbore
criticism. Even in her slight farces or old plays she seemed
rapidly to say, "How funny it is to break all the rules
and then pull out an indescribable bit of—well, what?
what would you call it?—out of this preposterous scene
like a rabbit or a scarf or a string of bells from an old
hat!" She eluded definition. Her old public failed to
describe her. *"Like no one else in the world!"* they
shouted, and repeated the charmed phrase in exasperation,
lacking another. Like the larger figures who had gone
before, like some of those who remained, she was dowered
with some overflow of wit or character or sparkling
presence that went beyond the boundaries of stage or
part. She played for six weeks to crowded houses, and at
the end for her benefit received tributes which completed
the cycle of reminiscence with a new touch of luxury: a
golden wreath for her hair, set with diamonds, and a
package filled with gold eagles.

Returning to the East after these triumphs Lotta produced a California play, *Heartsease, or What's Money
Without?* by Edmund Falconer. Small, farcical pieces on
the gold rush had been common enough in its early days,

and then had died out as their novelty waned. Credit for
the first full-length play of California mining life has
usually been given to Augustin Daly's *Horizon;* and by
an odd stroke its plot, unraveling the fortunes of a girl
who had been taken to the Coast by a worthless father, was
sometimes said to have a partial origin in the career of
Lotta. But with an initial performance in Boston in May,
1870, *Heartsease* was produced nearly a year before
Horizon, was quite as credible in plot, and inspired the
same comparisons with *The Luck of Roaring Camp.*

One writer said that *Heartsease* was built around a
banjo, and that the only shade of difference between the
play and a minstrel show was the shade of burnt cork: but
this was to wrong the muse of melodrama. The story
unrolls the career of May Wylderose, a young English
girl of gentle birth who is taken to California under improbable circumstances, and keeps a camp store, dispens-
ing food, whiskey, and moral advice to an assorted group
of miners, a typical Yankee—with a Yankee comedian's
part—a German, an Englishman, also of gentle birth and
slightly disguised, a Frenchman, and two knaves of un-
determined origin. Rough and peppery, ready with sharp
repartee, May has learned to play the favored banjo in
California, and to dance a clog or breakdown: truly
enough the scenes are lavishly interspersed with these
entertainments. She has also learned to take care of her-

self, and is prepared to take care of the well-born Englishman in time of trial. In a deep and secret cañon
where he has buried his store of gold he is beset by two
villains. High above, at the brink of the precipice, May
appears, armed with a speaking trumpet through which
she shouts, "Villains, forbear!" and fires two shots: but
the pair escape with the gold, leaving the hero bound
fast and all but dead in the depths of the gulch. The
precipice is high; May flings herself into the chasm by
a windlass, drops perilously down hand over hand, ties
her lover to a plank, and after skirting the cañon hauls
him up. After she has nursed him through the inevitable illness, and the Englishman inconsequently de-
parts, May shows her fortitude in a soliloquy (flute
tremolo) and at the same time absent-mindedly but
with her usual vigor begins digging the dirt floor with a
spade. She upturns an enormous nugget of pure gold. The
two villains, once more on the scene, who had been listening to the soliloquy and watching the excavation, rush for
the treasure. In the struggle which follows both are
tripped, May clutches two pistols, sits on the nugget,
neatly crosses a leg, and levels one revolver from her
knee, the other from the tip of her tiny foot. (Slow curtain.) In the final act wild May appears as a hoyden in
an English drawing-room, plays the banjo almost as
freely as in the mining camp, goes through many an odd

turn with a minstrel flavor, and puts to shame her affected rival, gradually learning meantime a new repertoire of pretty ways, and winning the hero.

The play ran for six weeks at Niblo's Garden, with men all but seated on the rafters. Lotta played *Heartsease* all over the country for two years, even in California, where she seems to have given it a wilder touch of extravaganza. Apparently she gave the whole piece in this mood. Melodrama, to merit its name, must overflow with large emotions. Lotta skirted them. "Piquant . . . freaks of fun and animal spirits . . . doing things that no one else could do," chimed the critics. She played her turbulent parts on a slight surface, with an elastic humor. Her pantomime with pistols—which she constantly varied— was said to be prodigal of comedy. With humor in pistols melodrama fled out of the window. At first the effect may have been unconscious: she created an excited, amused bravado of a kind which she had met abundantly in the mountains as a child, and struck something of the key of the miners' songs. She had hit upon this because it was familiar, in a play of gold rush days: but as the contagious fun spread she infused more and more of it into every piece of melodrama that she touched. Many of the endings of her acts or scenes in other plays were re-written to give scope for this fantastic combination.

Another uncalculated effect of *Heartsease, or What's Money Without?* appeared in the life of the Crabtrees.

Money was rolling in at an enviable rate; Lotta seemed
to have reached a new pinnacle of popularity. Yet Mrs.
Crabtree may have dwelt upon the faint pattern of the
plot. "What's money without?" she perhaps queried. The
family had been scattered; the boys were growing up;
England was ancestral. Mrs. Crabtree made a decision;
they would all go abroad. So the boys were put in an
English school, and Lotta went to Paris, where for some
months she studied French and painting, for which she
had a considerable aptitude, with a knack for catching
likenesses. She took lessons on the piano, and perhaps
pored over other polite arts. When the winter was over,
Mrs. Crabtree took a house in Cheshire, where the family
was united, and where Lotta bloomed out in white muslin
with blue ribbons, looked eighteen though she was nearly
twenty-seven, and drove a pony-cart. She looked indeed
like a young lady in a light novel of the time, and wrote
letters like one.

The Crabtrees remained in England for nearly a year.
Keeping the part of the airy young heroine, Lotta declined
to act in London, but she became the guest of the Lord
Mayor at a banquet at which were assembled all the
mayors of England and Wales; and presently, in the
American papers, she was reported dead or dying, which
proved again that she was famous. This notice may have
been a reminder. The holiday came to an end; Lotta laid

aside her new rôle, perhaps for use in the far future. For years afterward the Crabtrees indulged in no more romantic dreams. Lotta took her holidays in some obscure place in the country, for rest. The only immediate trace of her English trip appeared in double stereoscopic pictures for contemplation on Sunday afternoons, in which she was shown in dark silks and velvets with her pretty head tip-tilted against her hands, looking both pensive and elegant. The silks and velvets were strictly limited in number. In the first furor of Lotta's success in the East Mrs. Crab-tree had herself bloomed out in flowered brocade; but this gay garment was made over many times for Lotta. Mrs. Crabtree soon retreated to black, with a dark shawl and a close bonnet. Lotta's usual costumes were of equal plainness. They lived and traveled with an extreme economy.

Lotta plunged again into her roistering repertoire, danced more audaciously than ever, added a new break-down to her part as the Marchioness, and displayed a further skill with the snare-drum. The acrobatic song and dance was now in full swing. Flip-flops were the style. Though Lotta never fulfilled the technical rôle, her bold lively feats approached these novelties. She added min-strel business, put her hands near her hair to warm them, slipped her foot between the folds of a curtain when the applause lasted too long and stamped it, a gesture which was considered endlessly witty, and perhaps was, after the hilarious configurations of her dancing. Presently she came out in *Zip, or the Point Lynde Light,* which she played with her own admixture of melodrama and extravaganza with an acrobatic touch. In the opening scene the merry Zip bounds from a great fish-basket singing *Fishes and Crabs,* plays both the banjo and the hand-organ, and later comes upon the old lighthouse-keeper, her guardian, all but dead at the hand of wreckers. A ship bearing treasure—and Zip's unknown mother—is to strike the rocks, and indeed tacks into plain view on a practical sea with roaring waves in motion, rousing thunder, streaks of lightning, and the wrongfully lit flares of the wreckers off stage. Zip seizes a long rope of the breeches-buoy that hangs from a mast, and with a swift run out over the rocks flings herself across a deep and perilous strait. Landing with easy step at the door of the lighthouse, she lights the lamp, saves the ship, and through two remaining acts devotes her wit and tomboyish ways to the foiling of another set of villains, clambering through skylights and handling pistols with energy and comedy, and at last rising to love and fortune.

Most of Lotta's plays were written for her; she had innumerable small pieces like *The Rainbow,* a rapid farce which ran into minstrelsy and even legerdemain, with Lotta singing *Under the Daisies* and transforming herself into a character called Corduroy Bill, then into Persipio Boosey Buff, Esquire, a Tiger, and singing—

"I'm gwine away by the light of the moon,
    Want all the children for to follow me—
I hope I'll meet you darkies soon,
    Halle, Halle, Halle, hallelujah!

"So tell all the brothers that you meet,
    Want all the children for to follow me,
And that I will travel on my feet,
    Halle, Halle, Halle, hallelujah!

"In the morning by the bright light,
    Hear Gabriel's trumpet in the morning!"

Her voice was warm and full. She had the ample volume needed for such bold rhythms, and raced toward black-face comic opera.

She tried a version of *Jack Sheppard*—like Menken—but apparently the action was too desperate to lend itself to a touch-and-go burlesque, and she soon came out in a far slighter melodrama, *Musette*, which had the novelty of gypsy scenes. Her popularity ran to new heights. At New Orleans in the winter of 1874, in spite of financial stringency in the South and strong competition from other theatrical attractions she drew the largest houses of the season. In little towns of the Middle West she was met at the station more than once by admirers who took the horses from the shafts of her carriage and drew her in an enthusiastic mob to her hotel. She was a prime favorite in

Boston. All over the country she had made a widespread audience as intimately her own as had been the smaller public of the Sierras or of San Francisco.

Soon she was acting with Sothern, Mrs. John Drew, W. J. Florence, and others in a New York benefit for the unfortunate Edwin Adams, playing an act from *Othello*. Sothern faintly imposed the monocle and mincing step of Lord Dundreary upon Othello. Florence as Iago assumed an Irish brogue. Mrs. Drew played Emilia, with perhaps a touch of the Malaprop. And Lotta as Desdemona in a ball-gown, her hair looped in curls, frisked and tossed her train about, played ball with the pillows, with Iago joining in, and instead of the Willow Song gave a number on the banjo with a final breakdown. With Lotta in the lead—every one agreed that she gave the scene its impetus—the scene became minstrelsy, with Sothern hopping about, playing a distant, stuttering, lisping Othello, until Florence put an end to the scene with a fire-hose.

The performance was an index of the growing esteem in which Lotta was held by actors, and her place as a comedian. The same group played together for another benefit in Philadelphia. After these episodes Sothern wrote her a note which she thought kind and witty, saying that when she came on the stage the lights were brilliant, that when she went off "it seemed as if the gas were turned down," "and that I was so natural that I made all the rest seem like mere actors," as she happily declared. Jefferson told her that she had accomplished in a brief time what it had taken him years to learn, and meant the impalpable companionship which she at once established with an audience. She had the tribute of many actors; already —in the middle seventies—she was in the vanguard of a movement, though she bothered little about such matters, except as they brought her praise or pleasure.

Opprobrium was still heaped upon the stage. Lotta herself entered into a passionate defense of theater people against Talmadge. Yet in spite of the attacks of the ministry, in spite of a lingering prejudice, the theater was now in fine feather; as if in mockery of solemn strictures its most rebellious forms, minstrelsy and variety, had come into full life, with brief comic sketches, principally Irish or blackface, of the kind that Lotta had long since made her own. Harrigan, with whom she had played in San Francisco, had joined with Hart in a transcendent variety team. The San Francisco Minstrels, with whom she had made a hundred combinations, were enthroned in New York. Maggie Mitchell, who was sometimes compared with Lotta, had developed an original vein of high comedy with a personal accent of a wholly different order. Dozens of minor comedians from the same school were scattered over the country. Many of the crowd of minstrel and variety players were invading the legitimate theater, arousing the resentment of players in an older, staid tradition. Beginning underground, nour-

LOTTA AS BARNEY O'BRIEN

In "The Little Detective"

LOTTA. TWO PORTRAITS FROM THE '70's

ished in many an out-of-the-way theater on outlying
boundaries and on the ultimate frontier of the Pacific
Coast as well as in the larger theaters in New York, a
new and native extravaganza was becoming articulate.

In this insurgent movement Lotta was a gay pioneer.
She encircled the whole affair by a sweeping personal
gesture. She had learned her art early, in situations where
both life and the theater had been unrestrained, where a
new expansion on the stage had furthered a wild hilarity.
If she had few native plays, the whole underply of her
extravaganza was native with its strain of minstrelsy and
variety. What plays could she better have used in the
racketing drama of the time, still deeply overlaid by the
traditions of an antique English comedy? What other
parts could she have found as a comedian? No great burlesques were being written. No feminine lead in legitimate comedy could compare with the part of Colonel
Sellers in *The Gilded Age*. Most actresses of power
verged toward the lyric, or aspired toward Lady Audley.

From one view Lotta seemed like many other adventurers of the era who had flung themselves into the life
of one or another frontier, reaping a harvest of rich experience, and then in the fluctuant new life of the country
found themselves incomplete, with no ample medium in
which to use their talents. None of her plays seemed to
give full scope to her power. Yet perhaps she never truly
required more spacious plays than those in which she

could mix extravaganza and melodrama with her own special artistry. She seems to have been one of those personalities which belong to the theater but not to the drama, which will overpass any proper vehicle with lawless force. She broke the traditions of the stage; she broke traditions as to the place of women in life as well as in the theater. Already her sprightly destruction was having its effect. Lotta had her rivals and mimics, some of whom proved vexatious, copying her plays and stage business minutely. One critic declared that she was "the creator and chief representative of a school that was as well defined and as well understood in her day as was the school of the Kembles in their day, or the school of Garrick and Kean, who punctured inflated Kembleism." On large ground Lotta was giving impetus to a whole group of younger players, some of whom were to carry her free comedy to other realms on the stage. In the eighties young Minnie Maddern was hailed as another Lotta. "We were all imitating delightful Lotta in those days," said Mrs. Fiske many years later.

At a dozen points Lotta remained an originator, with novel triumphs, not only breaking traditions but inventing the surest way of sending these into limbo, that of laughter. The cry then and later was for native plays with a pictorial embodiment of American life. But perhaps more perishable materials were to prove deeply American. Keeping a pace which belonged to her own period, Lotta came to the brink of contemporary musical comedy, the blackface revue, of comic opera. She gave impetus to a form of fantasy in which native actors and composers and writers were to prove singularly adept. Perhaps this light and transient expression, appearing like fireworks, quickly dying, catching the changing color of the day, could never in itself endure. Yet it could be transmitted through years by the most definite artistic heritage—quickly as this seems to vanish—that of the stage, with a momentum which seemed to belong inalienably to Lotta's small figure, giving it a continued life.

VII

LOTTA

In the early eighties an old man clad in buckskin coat and trousers, with thick gray hair and a snowy beard, drifted into Sacramento after a fifteen days' ride from the mountains of Oregon. He was Wesley Venua, who had begun his career as an actor nearly fifty years before, and had uttered the opening lines at the initial performance given at one of the three Jenny Lind Theatres. His season there had been distinguished by quarrels with Maguire; he had afterward tried to establish a small theater in Sacramento on the novel principle of the joint stock company, where young Edwin Booth had joined him for a time; he had had a changing fortune as an actor in California for a dozen or more years. His later adventures had been endless, ranging from an idyllic passage in the South Seas to imprisonment as a soldier in the Franco-Prussian War; and he related these with small loss of theatrical effect. Honored for the diversion he now offered and for his legendary past, he was called the "histrionic pioneer."

Many such characters appeared on the Coast in these years. Tales of their strange risks and achievements were

part of a larger legend. One early actor had become a
Mormon preacher, just as an early Mormon had become
a California actor. Another had traveled through Washington giving solitary performances, and later turned up
as a potentate in Syria. Some had settled down to a rooted
life in the mountains, giving occasional entertainments,
no more to be dislodged than were case-hardened argonauts of the early days who still remained there and were
to last out their lives, prospecting. Jake Wallace was an
established favorite in the variety halls of San Francisco; for years his appearance was a signal for the shout,
"Forty-nine! Forty-nine!" At some point in his performance he would reel off *The Days of Forty-nine*, a
long ballad celebrating many excellent partners, which
had been composed by another early trouper on the Coast
who had come across the plains. All through the seventies
long trips by stage-coach were made by traveling actors
into the higher Sierras and into Washoe. Young Mr. and
Mrs. Bates had gone to Carson City and Pioche in winter,
driving into a snowstorm, beset by misfortune; two of
the horses were found to be dying and had to be left behind; with the remaining pair the company slowly limped
into Pioche through the bitter morning cold, Mrs. Bates
with a small baby in her arms. At night they played a
tragedy with the usual afterpiece. The domestic picture
was frequent; as in the earlier days players reared families in the midst of such travels; the women sewed, con-

trived costumes and properties, packed and unpacked the inevitable champagne baskets, and made a brief corner of a home in two lodging-house rooms or over the hall in which they played for a night.

A company which included Blanche and Ella Chapman, younger members of the famous Chapman family, Jake Wallace, and a few others, encountered highwaymen as they traveled through the mountains by stage-coach in the late seventies. Annoyed because their quarries were actors and could be expected to have small funds, the bandits forced the company out of the coach at the point of pistols and put them through a variety entertainment on the dusty road. Blanche Chapman danced. Ella, an accomplished banjoist, played with Wallace. A ventriloquist cast his trembling notes and funny sayings into waste spaces. There were songs and the lilt of merry-making in front of slitted black masks and heavy glistening barrels. The fastidious bandits then danced quadrilles and lancers with the ladies of the company. At last the company was permitted to resume its journey. After rapid coaching of perhaps twenty miles, the hardened stage-driver fainted. The treasure-box, which the bandits had neglected to examine, contained a fabulous sum, astutely placed there by a Wells-Fargo agent under the tacit protection of the troupe.

Young David Belasco was basket-boy at the Metropolitan when Mr. and Mrs. Bates were there. Later he formed an alliance with the resilient Maguire, who at the rise of the California Theatre had repeated his old rôle of the imperturbable gambler, borrowing a thousand dollars from a barkeeper and indulging his old passion for minstrelsy with handsome luck. He had brought Billy Emerson to the Coast, perhaps the most popular single minstrel player of any period, and entrenched Emerson's company there for many a long year. Striding forward, securing a millionaire patron of his own, Maguire had soon opened the Baldwin Theatre, and raced the California for place with another excellent stock company of which young Belasco became a member. All the old strains —of legitimate theatricals, opera, minstrelsy, variety— were now abroad in San Francisco with full vigor, as if each with its changing career had taken deep root. New theaters were springing up in number, removed from the old colorful purlieus of Portsmouth Square, but with rivalries running higher than ever. Lines were stretched across the continent.

Traditions reached forward through decades. Many years later Belasco rounded the cycle of gold rush plays with *The Girl of the Golden West,* starring Blanche Bates, daughter of the Mr. and Mrs. Bates who had fought Maguire and joined the pioneer troupers. Jake Wallace was included as a character in the play; and in the Coast production Wallace was invited to play Wallace. His lines were brief. A few mirthful spirits among old troupers urged him to improve upon them. Keeping other actors in the wings at the first performance, Wallace marched down to the front of the stage and gave a banjo number with all the innumerable verses of his ballad. But the enlarged episode, which might have been accepted in the flexible earlier days, failed to fit into a carefully oiled production, and was not repeated.

In that shadowy and passing world of the theater, so brilliantly lit for a time, so broken and insubstantial, a whole body of players was etched out in strong character, whose history, like Lotta's, reached back toward the first rich history of the stage in California. Continuity was there, as individuals and companies surged together and still wove a common life out of strands of plays or action or the fortunes of the road. This world grew solid through the interchanges which were part of its character, through tradition or fresh departures from tradition, through theatrical families like the Chapmans, whose younger members were coming forward, or through long lives like that of Maguire.

Lotta Crabtree skimmed lightly through that impalpably knit society. She went to the Coast again and again for engagements, played under the management of Maguire at the Baldwin with young Belasco in the cast, gave her famous fountain to the city of San Francisco, a reminiscence of mountain days in its care for thirsty horses, then feared that her gift would be con-

strued as a bid for favor and declined to act there for a
time. She visited the mountain camps where she had
played as a child; she often spent brief holidays in California; soon she was appearing in San Francisco again in
new plays. But she continually slid away; few of her personal relationships seemed deep or enduring. Most of her
associations on the stage were slight.

She was often supported by interesting figures of the
stage, Mrs. Gilbert, Stuart Robson, Crane, Thomas Whif-
fen, young Adah Rehan. Her association with Mrs. John
Drew was long and pleasant. Lotta was amiable with other
actors; she lacked arrogance; her companies liked her. If
her houses failed to reach their usual scale she thought
the fault was hers; when they overflowed she called the
company together and thanked them. Occasionally she
slipped aside from the routine of rehearsal and production for small hilarities. But these too were highly transient. Her support was constantly being altered; she must
have played with hundreds of actors within a few years,
at first joining with local companies when she was on
tour, later, from 1880 onward, when she had her own
company, still playing with a large and changing number.
Her own rôle was the only large or taxing one in most
of her plays; she failed to draw superior talent for any
length of time. Even her mode of production kept her
at a distance from other actors. She rehearsed her companies but did not rehearse with them. She was emphatic

in saying that she did not care to have them know precisely what she was going to do; with her usual freedom she frequently changed the detail of her action, and thus succeeded in keeping her plays in the realm where she wanted them, that of spontaneity. But the scheme, free in its effects, was haphazard for the company, and seemed secret.

Certain outlines of Lotta's fate were becoming plain. She was as aloof from small and homely companionships as she had been as a child: she still had on a prodigious scale the companionship of the crowd, with high-colored personal tributes. During one of her engagements in New Orleans the Grand Duke Alexis, ravished by her acting, presented her with a set of bracelets and a necklace set with diamonds and turquoises and handsomely chased, and gave a dinner in her honor on board a Russian warship during which each officer was permitted to sit at her side for ten minutes. Handsome jewelry was her steady toll, as it was for other popular actresses in a lavish day. Managers gave her pretty lockets. On one of her western trips she was entertained by that early patron of the stage, Brigham Young. The proverbial crowd around the stage-door was dense; Lotta was the idol of hundreds of young men of the seventies and eighties, who seldom obtained more than a glimpse of her as she sped in and out of the theater. A few were luckier; since she maintained her air of incredible innocence whatever she did, somehow she

made her way into assemblages where actresses seldom
penetrated, and even went to private balls during some
of her longer sojourns in middle western cities, and had
a semblance of a belle's gay time. Yet these agreeable
interludes were brief; she invariably set out again on the
road with her long routine of travel and sleep, coming
down to dinner in blue serge, taking a bowl of crackers
and milk after the theater, living in unpretentious rooms.
Occasionally, her mother, who still controlled the details
of business management, took an apartment when their
stay in a city was to be long enough; the whole family
would be united, with the two boys in the group and occasionally joining in managership or walking on.

They were an engaging family during such passages,
the boys wild, careless, gay, full of odd tales; even Crabtree had his fine moments; and Mrs. Crabtree, with her
photographic memory and mimicry, capped the group. But
for the most part Lotta's two brothers were off on errands
of their own; in any case the long cycle of travel remained. At times Lotta drove furiously after the theater
with her mother until daylight, unable to wear off the
tension of playing. One afternoon in a small western town
she drove about for hours in a hack through a storm with
water and mud up to the hubs. Some one remembered
seeing her curled up at the end of a railway coach alone
and forlorn, smoking surreptitiously during a long journey. She sometimes smoked as furiously as she drove,

smoked black cigars. Modjeska, who was deeply impressed by Lotta's originality and talent, found her intense and highly strung.

But another pattern was positive in that oddly detached existence. Whatever the monotony of years, Lotta failed to show their burden. She remained young, fresh, and flexible in her dancing and in her humor. Once she had passed the barrier of the wings she became the brilliantly animated small figure which her audiences had learned to expect; her merriment seemed unstrained. She continued to create new bits of action and production; she put on new plays of the hoydenish school. Her *Ma'amzelle Nitouche* was all but comic opera, with Lotta in a Japanese rôle which anticipated later productions, scudding about the stage in a kimono with a pink lampshade on her head pretending to light up dark corners, and with her favorite doubling and dash of the military. She produced *La Cigale* in an extravagant version, and repeated the effect of her slighter early melodramas in *Pawn Ticket 210*. The critics were harsh in their notices of this piece; its young authors, Belasco and Clay Greene, wished it withdrawn. But Lotta, for whom it was written, gave the play an infectious life, and turned it into a popular success almost on the instant with a queue for tickets stretching around four sides of a Chicago theater.

Playing in England at the end of the eighties, she met a severe test. The most hard-working and assiduous of

her imitators had learned of the proposed trip, had has-
tened over before her, and had launched many of Lotta's
favorite parts. When Lotta appeared, their positions were
reversed: Lotta was considered the imitator. She had besides the misfortune of choosing an incompetent manager;
indeed the season was full of mischance. An actor who
had recently secured a divorce was in the company; and
British principles came to the fore. To cap disaster, Lotta
opened in *Musette,* whose scene was English and contained a passage in which a wicked baronet pursues an
innocent girl. The play, taken seriously, was considered
outmoded. Apparently Lotta was unable to reach the full
flood of her extravagant handling of the piece; or her
innovations were misunderstood. Every word of the play
was interrupted, every actor hissed, including Lotta herself; the noise in the theater became a tempest; the curtain went down long before the play was over. She took
the episode as she had taken the rebel demonstrations
long before on her wagon tour of Oregon during the
Civil War. Undaunted, she played *Little Nell and the
Marchioness* the next night. The move was courageous,
because her rival had preëmpted the part, and because
Dickens had seldom been played in England with lavish
embellishments of minstrelsy and burlesque. But Lotta's
courage held something more than temper or daring;
apparently she possessed momentum and control. Her
humor slid over its light surface; she infused the part of

the Marchioness with its essential pathos. This time the audience was merely cold. She repeated the play, and gradually won a startled enthusiasm. "Lotta's Marchioness is a performance *sui generis*," admitted a leading critic. "It is the quaintest, oddest conception in the world, and though it may be heresy to say so, her breakdown is the funniest thing ever done in comic dancing. . . . Lotta's face as she sits on the kitchen table, eyeing the dreadful mutton-bone, haunts me. No words can describe the fantastic tricks of this actress." In the end, by sheer high spirits and subtle adaptation, she transformed an almost abysmal failure into something like success.

Where did it come from, that wellspring of lively fun and mounting airy vivacity? What kept it full and over-flowing? On she had gone, for nearly thirty years, with undiminished comic force. In those early tours long ago in the mountains had she caught some deep humor or wild assurance, a surcharged gayety which was to last for a lifetime? Or had she found an obscure capacity for pleasure deeply caught within herself? She had kept it in spite of a narrowing personal experience, without the brush and stimulus of fresh contacts. A sense of humor is sometimes developed in comparative solitude, a sense of fun or broad comedy almost never. Was her temperament simple? Many persons thought so: off-stage she was said to be a charming but not always an interesting companion. Yet the hundreds of her photographs—she was perhaps the most fully pictured actress of her time—suggest another story.

As with her voice, something of richness or amplitude was there beyond an apparent character. Her moods were so radical that they colored whole groups of photographs of a single sitting: even as a child the effect had been clear. Some of her pictures were full of the most energetic strength, with the sweeping odd outline of her eyes and eyebrows firmly drawn, her eyes so black that they seemed dark dagger-points. At other times she was delicate and pensive, or solidly matter-of-fact. She was wistful; often she merely posed, and posed well. Witchery appeared, which may have been a little wasted, as in faint colors, with an adornment of white fur, her little hat tiptilted, she looked delicately downward, holding in one hand a black and smoking cigar, the emblem of her histrionic and personal rebellion. One photograph of later years, at full length, shows her as though she had been suddenly caught in a moment of graceful and appealing humor, with a touch of personal emotion which seldom appeared in her likenesses or in her acting. She seemed about to step into a pleasing social comedy.

Something prisoned was suggested in all that amplitude—wild orbits contained within herself like her passionate temper, with a sweetness and tenderness which could hardly emerge in her boisterous comedy. Hers was an odd fate. Though her companionship with her audi-

ences was so wide that it was often discussed as the outcome of a deep and special gift, she lacked personal companionship almost altogether. All her life, from childhood, she had been surrounded by crowds, and also by
powerful, intriguing personalities. Within her own com-
pass she too possessed an unmistakable power, which never
came to an entire fruition. One sees her through years, at
first all but overwhelmed as she passed among greater
figures, then gradually emerging in her own right, but
becoming more and more solitary with all her iridescent
charm, as she traveled down the decades.

Change came at last, when in 1891 Lotta retired from
the stage. There were many rumors. It was true that she
had been ill; but she had recovered. A few people thought
that her difficulties in England had broken her confidence;
but these had been overcome, and she had been received
again in this country with her accustomed high favor.
Soon after her withdrawal Belasco planned to bring her
back; the arrangements were well developed; apparently
for a time she intended to return. Perhaps she wished to
remain on the stage; obviously she was drawn by the life
of the theater. She was still in early middle age. But she
did not return; afterwards she declared that she had
decided to leave while her popularity still endured.

As always, in her long career, there was an effect of
timeliness in her decision, something as exquisitely precise as the pattern contained within her roughest dancing.

MARY ANN CRABTREE

A portrait from the '80's

LOTTA. A PORTRAIT FROM THE '80's

Her personal vogue might have continued for years: but the assault of the critics on *Pawn Ticket 210* had had significance; the day was passing when the rude light structure of most of Lotta's plays could pass muster, even with the original life and coloring which she gave them. The interest in Dickens, so deeply rooted from the forties onward, was beginning to diminish. Minstrelsy, Lotta's native field, had undergone a complete change. The older minstrelsy, full of small rich parts and a full characterization, had all but vanished in the nineties. The new order had been foreshadowed by the monstrous lettering that advertised Haverly's—40—Count Them—40—and by the silken parti-colored costumes that blackface performers now often assumed. Burlesque had become something that bore little relation to its name, and was now a dubious affair of chorus-girls in tights. If the drift in the theater was toward a large number of native plays and closer dramatic forms, its comic entertainment was showier, less essentially daring, less humorous. Lotta's boisterous art would soon have been out of date; or, if one prefers, the time for her modern low comedy had not yet come.

Lotta now came into riches like the worthy small heroine of many of her plays. Prim as Mrs. Crabtree had looked in those early precarious years in the far West, she had apparently caught a touch of the gambling instinct. Still prim in her plain bonnets, as she had traveled through the country with Lotta year after year, she had surveyed every scene, had marched out through half-built sections of new cities and had purchased lots. She might have carried a divining rod for wealth under her cloak; she seemed to know by instinct that an unpromising site would eventually turn into money. Many of these risky chances had long since been fabulously transformed; and there was besides the large accumulated capital from box-office receipts. All of Mrs. Crabtree's arrangements had been close. Her early need for thrift had left a lasting print upon her character; all her genius for management had turned toward the accumulation of wealth, once the first routine of Lotta's career was assured. She drove hard bargains with playwrights, and almost invariably bought Lotta's plays for a flat sum, so there were no royalties to pay when success was achieved. With managers too, or companies, she had made narrow contracts; and in her management of her own and Lotta's personal affairs she had remained frugal, though in these later years, as their wealth began to take on unmistakable bulk and area, she had donned the bugles which were a fashion of the time for headgear, and wore the black dazzling ornaments with a firm air of triumph. After all, her accomplishment was hardly meager. Half a century before she had entered the rush for gold with thousands of others; though all the odds were against her she had gained a foothold, with Lotta, and in the end a fortune: it was something to have succeeded where ten thousand men had failed or had thrown their luck away. There had long been the distinct aura of gold about the Crabtrees, frugally as they had lived. They had it. Their wealth could be counted in millions.

But the world of the theater which they now left behind had been Lotta's only world, where she had seemed to bloom into a new and special life of her own. It had been her mother's great vocation. What would they do away from it? How would they live? How would they make a life, these somewhat solitary people? What would it come to, that half century of oblique changes, sudden fun, and endless money-getting? They had many theatrical relationships, hundreds of acquaintances, few close friends, perhaps no intimacies. Marriage for Lotta was out of the question. The newspapers had carried stories of romance about her, but these had been thin little pieces, spun out of knowledge of the admiration which she commanded and the effort to make a tiny sensation. For a brief time she had been engaged to a young army officer, who had died; a few other small affairs had claimed her. Spectators of the lives of the Crabtrees—and with their travels these were legion—were inclined to attribute to her mother her failure to marry. But in Lotta's compact temperament was a strain of fickleness, something as light as her changing humor, or at least the capacity to make sudden intense reversals; it is doubtful whether any of these interests occupied her for long.

Lotta and Mrs. Crabtree had made a simple scale of values their own, one frequently observed in native literature and on the stage, and even more often in the contemporary life through which they had made their way. After early privation and hard work they meant to enjoy luxury, and did, with peculiar pleasure. In the prospect which spread out before them a single flaw appeared in the figure of Crabtree. He had lived for years on the fringe of their existence: now—did they after all regret the end?—he withdrew, went to England, and died there soon after his arrival. Almost at once Mrs. Crabtree built a spacious summer home on the shore of a lake in the New Jersey hills, with pretty gables, wide verandas, and sloping green lawns: here with Lotta she settled for something like country life for many months in the year. Lotta—now once more Miss Lotta—bought a few race-horses for her brother Ashworth; she herself drove a spirited pair. The two boys, handsome young men, indulged in sports after the fashion of young Englishmen of wealth, and occasionally were with them. They all drew into their circle a changing group of friends or acquaintances whom they saw with transient pleasure much as they had enjoyed brief encounters during their years of travel.

Theirs was a pleasant household, with light surfaces and easy contacts. Lotta was as inordinately fond of masquerades as she had been of doubling on the stage; she gave innumerable impromptu parties. A friendly satirist, she mimicked actors she had known, or her acquaintances: her portrayals, as slight but as clearly drawn as vivid pencil sketches, had neither envy nor bitterness. She went through whole scenes from her plays, dragged out her costumes, even the ragged ones—these indeed most frequently of all—and returned again and again to her rôle as the Marchioness. In spite of her many declarations that she never missed the stage, she seemed not to tire of these dramatic recollections. For the rest, she painted—painted herself in character, most often as the Marchioness, studying the part in a mirror and achieving a quick veracity in the likeness. She drifted off with her easel and sketched landscapes like the young lady in a polite novel which she had learned to be in England many years before, and was miraculously convincing in the light part. She was forty-four when she left the stage; at fifty and much later her appearance of youth became a subject for minor fable. With her red curls, her clear black eyes, her swift movements, she looked an agreeable twenty-five or thirty; in white muslin with a blue sash she was girlish. An effect of strain which had sometimes appeared in the immense gallery of her photographs had gone; the odd bias of her character came out with graceful force. "Watch her sudden squirrel-like ways and you would expect to hear a shallow-voiced chatter," said a companion for an hour, who was continually surprised by "that warm voice of hers that never seemed to fit her." Her voice still hinted an enigma of temperament; even on the quiet sparkling surface on which she lived a slight oddity appeared. She was absorbed in her old parts; she was defensive about comedy, and even became contentious when the subject came up, declaring that comedy was far harder to achieve than any other form of acting. Yet except for this emphasis she seemed to slip away from the memory of her career. Many of its episodes she totally forgot in the course of years.

Mrs. Crabtree forgot nothing. She was the *raconteur*, holding her listeners enthralled as she told story after story of adventures as she had traveled with Lotta in the mountains, as she mimicked or described the striking figures they had known. She was terse; her thrift extended to words. Her voice, far more emotional than Lotta's, boomed or rolled or softened as she narrated her strange episodes. She had her firm opinions. She was still heartily loyal to the memory of Lola Montez. Likewise Adah Menken came into friendly life again under her quick touch. She talked of Mart Taylor, with whom they had made their first tour in the mountains, and of Jake Wallace, who had taught Lotta to play the banjo. Nor was it only the more conspicuous characters that she remembered: on the first voyage out, in jaunts about the mines, in stage-coaches or at small hotels, she had seen dozens of men and women whose history she had heard in part, whom she had seen in the midst of high-colored situations, and whom she sharply remembered. She was a matchless compendium of life in California during the fifties and sixties. She had other chapters, on her own experiences and Lotta's when they had traveled in the South after the War. Actors who had seen her sitting bolt upright in darkened theaters during rehearsals would have been astonished to know how much she had observed. She often used to carry a gingham apron to the theaters at night when she was on tour with Lotta, and after the performance would tie it around her waist, scoop the receipts into it and roll them up, bearing away this improvised money-belt. She told this; her past was never embellished.

She too was defensive about comedy. "It's life," she asserted with emphasis as in earlier days, and perhaps herself illustrated the circumstance. If Mrs. Crabtree had been lonely during those years of hard travel and meager living, no one would have guessed it. Perhaps she never was. She had Lotta. She had besides an imperturbable, balanced humor which made her take buffet after buffet and keep in view and in memory every touch of life in the immediate scene. So obscure, in the background for years, she had perhaps the richer talent of the two, and may have poured much of this into her child's life, shaping its mold, even providing the essential momentum for Lotta's comedy. Lotta herself frequently declared that she owed her entire career to her mother. "In myself I had no confidence," she said.

Her devotion—their common devotion—was unmistakable. The bond between Lotta and her mother was close —too close, too confining, even mysterious, some observers said—but there was no sign that it chafed. Perhaps Lotta had been swept into her career by Mrs. Crabtree's will; her life in consequence may have been narrowed or cramped. Yet this choice had given her in abundance possibilities which she had deeply enjoyed: there was no doubt of her special pleasure once she appeared before the footlights. Now they were both enjoying good fruits, less in their wealth than in the power to be themselves with extraordinary simplicity. One singular difference between them became clear in these shared passages of their later lives. Lotta had remained young: her mother had grown old far before her time; she looked old, even at times deeply troubled. As the years passed, in appearance she still sped quickly beyond them. A year or two before she died, in 1905, her sad and wrinkled face might have been that of Lotta's great-grandmother.

Ashworth Crabtree then joined his sister. Her brother George had died at sea some years earlier. Lotta's interest in horses increased. She had been a magnificent rider since childhood; her pleasure in racing had begun long ago on the Coast. She now enlarged her stables at Squantum and kept a string. One year her favorite, Sonoma Girl, won the Transylvania sweepstakes; another season she put in the best green pacer. "What do I like about horses?" she asked. "Why, gameness is the chief quality I admire in them. But of course speed counts. . . . I love to see the beautiful things flash by so swiftly mile after mile and all without apparent effort."

Lotta enjoyed these diversions for only a brief interval. She was alone after her brother Ashworth's death; and there were penalties attached to inexperience. That rich energy which she could still command had to find a channel; it turned, as her mother's had turned, to the accumulation of wealth. She became a little suspicious, and more than frugal. She feared that new acquaintances sought her out because she had been famous or because she was rich. Yet she kept a warm responsiveness for her small circle of friends; her humor was still quick and infectious. Once as a very old woman she slipped and fell, dangerously enough, in a Boston street. "Prima donna in the gutter!" she cried to her companion, and laughed as at a bit of old slapstick.

Wearing rich costumes of earlier years, still rapid of movement, she looked like the leading character in the revival of an old play. At times she became feverishly eager to have many people about her. "I want to go away where there are many people. I cannot exist without many around me," she insisted. She lived in her own hotel in

Boston, and remained essentially solitary. At times she would dress with antique resplendence, cover herself with jewels, and dine in state alone. Away for a summer season at Gloucester she was still much alone, even though she was a subject for friendly admiration. She was often late for appointments or far too early, as if it were her fate not to meet people precisely, though the fault may have been that of one of her many watches, tokens of her long popularity, which perhaps had suffered as time-pieces by a too enthusiastic transit to the stage. She had kept them, just as she had kept a box of gold nuggets from her California days.

At Gloucester she wandered about sketching. She still often painted herself, again at times as the Marchioness. Dressed in the familiar rags—she had treasured them—she sat before a mirror and tried to convey on canvas the one character of all her characters which had had the most breadth and the most pathos. Her fondness for the part had remained intense. She seemed to remember herself best as that funny, sad, irrepressible little outcast. One wonders what she thought as she peered into the silver surface, as she looked into her own black eyes and scrutinized that small pointed face with its frame of unruly red hair. She still kept to an amazing extent the appearance of youth. But she was old at last, and knew it; she hated old age. She was remembered; honor came to her in San Francisco at a celebration of early days on the Coast. To many people she seemed the positive embodiment of a glittering era. She joined in the festivities; she was happy but tired. She came back to Boston, lived more and more quietly, and died in 1924, well toward eighty.

Her death was followed by a strange scramble. Her wealth might have been placer gold spread to view in some rich gulch in the Sierras. Many persons considered themselves entitled to it. Gold might perhaps be had for the asking. Nearly a hundred claimants, most of them with the slenderest pretensions to acquaintance or relationship with Lotta, came forward. After the first judicial hearings most of these were eliminated from the contest over the will. Two claimants were permitted to press their cases. One of these declared that she was the daughter of Ashworth Crabtree by a common-law marriage, born during wild days at Tombstone, when he had wandered about without a tether. In a quiet Boston court, roaring days in Tombstone were brightly pictured. Characters, episodes, passed in a brief kaleidoscope; witnesses came from that old frontier; a final witness came from the Carolina mountains, with an account of a deathbed narrative by Crabtree, in which he had said that he had never had a child. Both cases revived the color of frontier life; in an extraordinary fashion both dredged up many of the remaining evidences of that older period; and the claim which concerns this history, that of the woman who maintained that she was Lotta Crabtree's daughter, offered as well a fabric of early melodrama. Her story might have been founded upon one of Lotta's old and least substantial plays. It hinged upon a question of mysterious parentage, with "papers" and tokens, and finally the disposal of a fortune. Perhaps the new plot was actually concocted from a remembrance of rude dramas performed long ago in shaky theaters of small towns in the Middle West, or on show-boats that tied up for a night at some tiny wharf on the Mississippi.

Ironically enough, this story presupposed a hidden passage in the open life of Mrs. Crabtree. The claimant attempted to prove that Lotta's mother had contracted a marriage which had preceded her marriage to John Crabtree, with another Crabtree said to be his cousin, John Edward. Lotta was described as the child of this union, born after a separation. John Edward was declared to have migrated to Illinois, where after another marriage he had reared a large family in a primitive cabin near Stringtown at Crabtree Ford, a desolate and lonely place facing west on the Mississippi. Bits of family drama were developed in this prelude. Mrs. Crabtree, according to the tale, insisted upon money payments from John Edward Crabtree. His wife, learning of the earlier tie, mixed "a potion of poison" and was saved from self-destruction only by the swift action of the claimant, who dashed the china cup from her hands. In the shallow narrative that followed this second wife was made to turn kindly toward Lotta in her time of trial.

According to the major story Lotta Crabtree was married secretly in England on Christmas Eve, 1877, to an unknown George Manning at "Crabtree Château," "the old ancestral home of the Crabtrees" in Lancashire. Manning was said to have disappeared in a few months; a child was declared to have been born "in the lap of luxury. . . . But the mother in great sorrow brought her to the home of John E. and Ann Jane Crabtree at Crabtree Ford in Illinois." These phrases, part of a terse outline of events, appeared in a worn Bible which was introduced as evidence. Lotta was pictured as traveling the considerable distance between Crabtree Château and Crabtree Ford, arriving one day at the cabin with her child in her arms and announcing, "I am Lotta Crabtree, the actress, and this is my child." Opportunely—in the story— the Crabtrees there had lost an infant girl by death only a day or two earlier; and the child which the shadowy Lotta thus brought to their door was taken into the family and reared as their own. There were, however, mysterious differences, as in a romantic play; this child had fine clothing, a saddle horse, gold bracelets; she was sent to school. She excited the envy of her foster brothers and sisters, and sometimes their jealous bitterness; she was in fact like Mabbie, or the foundling in *Pawn Ticket 210*, a child of trials. But at least she became the claimant, and was able to describe Miss Lotta as paying her many brief visits through later years, showering her with money and gifts, writing her many letters, taking her on long trips. During this period she declared that she had believed Lotta to be her half-sister. It was only after Lotta's death that the Bible containing the brief unhappy story came to light; Lotta was said to have given it long before to another member of the Crabtree family. Unopened, unread, the Bible had been placed in a chest, where it had lain until mention of Lotta's death had appeared in the public prints.

In the trial it turned out that all the letters which might have been proof of Lotta's association with the claimant had been burned in a recent fire. Every witness who had been present at those dim meetings was dead; and a dramatic conflict developed among the plaintiff's brothers and sisters as to her elaborate narrative. She was supported by some of them: but an older brother, with a marked combination of embitterment and veracity, made the journey from Crabtree Ford to Boston, and emphatically denied the entire supposition that the claimant was not his sister. Behind the struggle for truth in court appeared a dramatic anterior struggle in the family, likewise for truth or against it, which had involved a midnight ride by the claimant, another Bible which had been lost or stolen, and an effort to cover up or to reveal the date of John Edward Crabtree's birth, which was in fact far too late to have made possible the prelude of Mrs. Crabtree's first marriage. With the weaving and inter-weaving of testimony the case became immensely compli-cated; through the scale of the claims and by the fantastic evidence it reached a level that invited comparison with the case of the famous Tichborne claimant. Witnesses came forward in crowds for both sides, some with amaz-ing tales, as from persons who asserted that they had seen Lotta in England near Crabtree Château, presumably, at the time of her supposed marriage, or had heard Mrs. Crabtree talking back-stage in a western theater about Lotta's sorrows.

The ring of coin was audible throughout the trial, the glitter of gold all but visible. Money was declared to have been Lotta's repeated gift to the claimant. The jin-gle of gold and silver might perhaps have been heard at no great distance as some of the witnesses gave their strange testimony. By an odd involvement a recent gold rush, to the Oklahoma oil fields, was drawn into the trial through an explanation of the claimant's other enterprises. But confronted on the witness stand by a characteristic picture of Lotta, she was unable to say who it was. In a hasty moment, she admitted that she had given her hair a brassy tone to make it resemble Lotta's. The keystone of her pretensions was the old Bible with its long entry, purporting to outline the circumstances of Lotta's mar-riage and the birth of her child. An expert declared that the handwriting in which the entry was made bore an unmistakable resemblance to that of the claimant. The ink appeared to have been treated to make it take on the look of age. The covers showed signs of recent damage.

After years many details of Lotta's career had dropped from sight. She had kept no record of her tours. Because of her constant travel a precise outline of dates which could contradict the story was difficult to establish. But as knowledge of the preposterous claim spread, old memories were revived. Early playbills were discovered; old theater-goers and actors came forward. Proof was offered that Lotta was playing in New York and in Rochester on the two crucial dates of the supposed marriage and the birth of the child. This proof took on a charming quality, from its origin, casting a slight glow over a sordid scene. Lotta's career was faintly sketched, with remembered traces of the great affection in which she had been held by her public. As this testimony grew the case collapsed by its own incredible weight.

The will which the gold-seekers tried to break had a noticeable character. Over half of Lotta Crabtree's fortune was given to a foundation for the relief of needy veterans of the Great War; she provided for the care of sick in hospitals, and for prisoners on their emergence into the world; she left money for an actors' relief fund; she created a fund for students of music, another for students of agriculture, for good cheer at Christmas, and for

the promotion of laws against vivisection. She left money
for the care of worn-out horses and stray dogs. The
strands of many genuine interests appeared in her will:
but an outstanding circumstance was clear. She made only
a few small personal bequests. There could be no doubt
that she preferred not to share that great heap of money
—nearly four million dollars—with people whom she
knew. The bulk of her estate went to strangers. The provisions were complicated; one hates to think of her toiling
over them. It was perhaps a pity that her money had to
be disposed of at all; her fortune should have become a
legend like her mirth. Yet logic remains in that final
document, from Lotta, who seldom bothered about logic.
There was fitness in the circumstance that she gave her
great rewards to strangers. From strangers she had gained
them; and she seemed to have only conventional reasons
for personal bequests. Few persons had become an essential part of her life, out of the multitudes she had known.

Pathos appears in the long view of Lotta Crabtree's
life: yet it is only by artifice that her isolation may be
deeply stressed. Truly enough, her personal career had
been oddly accented; she had remained singular and detached, though she had lived since childhood close to a
thronging and insurgent existence, and had all but mixed
with many crowds. She had been lonely, but, when all the
years are counted, perhaps not too often. Besides the fundamental relationship in which she had found happiness,

she had had endless hours of sheer high amusement on the stage. In an extraordinary measure gayety had been her portion. Perhaps if her personal pleasure had been of a wider order some of this might have been dispersed; it had continued to well up as from some narrow source, pristine and untouched. With a wider experience her complete naturalness might have been lost; the quality may have been perfect because it was unassailed. So her will, with its effect of withdrawal, its survey of distances, may stand as an emblem of a long and bright efflorescence. If this pattern from one view seems to swerve from usual outlines, we may remember that the most balanced human patterns do not always possess great enchantment.

INDEX

257